THE EVIL EYE

by Guy Lyon Playfair

Guy Lyon Playfair

THE EVIL EYE
The Unacceptable Face
of Television

JONATHAN CAPE
LONDON

First published 1990
© Guy Lyon Playfair 1990
Jonathan Cape Ltd, 20 Vauxhall Bridge Road, London sw1v 2sa

A CIP catalogue record for this book
is available from the British Library

isbn 0–224–02791–3

Phototypeset by Falcon Graphic Art Ltd
Wallington, Surrey
Printed in Great Britain by
Mackays of Chatham plc

A small boy asleep on his right side, the right arm stuck out, the right hand hanging limply over the edge of the bed. Through a round grating in the side of a box a voice speaks softly.

'The Nile is the longest river in Africa and the second in length of all the rivers of the globe. Although falling short of the length of the Mississippi-Missouri, the Nile is at the head of all rivers as regards the length of its basin, which extends through 35 degrees of latitude . . .'

At breakfast the next morning, 'Tommy,' someone says, 'do you know which is the longest river in Africa?' A shaking of the head. 'But don't you remember something that begins: The Nile is the . . .'

'The-Nile-is-the-longest-river-in-Africa-and-the-second-in-length-of-all-the-rivers-of-the-globe . . .' The words come rushing out. 'Although-falling-short-of . . .'

'Well now, which is the longest river in Africa?'

The eyes are blank. 'I don't know.'

'But the Nile, Tommy.'

'The-Nile-is-the-longest-river-in-Africa-and-second . . .'

'Then which river is the longest, Tommy?'

Tommy bursts into tears. 'I don't know,' he howls.

Aldous Huxley, Brave New World

CONTENTS

ACKNOWLEDGMENTS

For providing me with research material, my thanks go to Pearl Coleman, Dr Crisetta MacLeod-Morgan, Dr Thomas Neuman, Professor David P. Phillips, Rex Research of Berkeley, California, and Dr Marcello Truzzi; also to the staff of the British Library's document supply centre, the Kensington and Chelsea Library, the psychology and periodicals sections of the University of London Library, and the Science Museum Library.

I am grateful to: Baillière Tindall Ltd for permission to quote an extract from *A Handbook of Medical Hypnosis* by Gordon Ambrose and George Newbold; the estate of the late Sonia Brownell Orwell and Secker & Warburg for permission to quote from *Nineteen Eighty-Four* by George Orwell; and to Mrs Laura Huxley and the Hogarth Press for permission to quote from *Brave New World* by Aldous Huxley.

Once again I am indebted to Tony Colwell for his ruthless but always constructive editing. Finally, my special thanks to Jerry Mander for allowing me to use the extract from his letter quoted in Chapter 3, for saving me from the Evil Eye and thereby providing the inspiration for this book.

Guy Lyon Playfair

PART ONE

If both the past and the external world exist
only in the mind, and if the mind itself is
controllable, what then?

George Orwell, *Nineteen Eighty-Four*

[He] left the room with a swagger, exulting,
as he banged the door behind him, in the
thought that he stood alone embattled against
the order of things, elated by the intoxicating
consciousness of his individual significance
and importance. Even the thought of
persecution left him undismayed, was rather
tonic than depressing.

Aldous Huxley, *Brave New World*

I

I CHOOSE FREEDOM

'Television rots the brain,' I said. 'We should have less of it, not more.'

Mine was not an original proposition, but the circumstances in which I made it were unusual. I was in a television studio in London recording a programme in the popular BBC series *Choices* to be screened the following Sunday evening. It had all started five or six weeks previously, when a friend of mine appeared as a panellist on an earlier programme in the series and sent me a studio audience ticket. I sat at the back and clapped obediently whenever the assistant held up the CLAP board, but during the discussions my mind began to wander, coming to rest on the card I had been handed inviting me to suggest a subject for a future programme.

I decided to propose that television was something we would all be better off without, and to my surprise I was called a few days later by the *Choices* researcher and told that my suggestion had been accepted. In due course, after a pleasant meeting with him and his colleagues, I learned that I was to be allowed to tell the nation's television viewers that they ought to be doing something else. So here I was.

With me on the stage were Mary Kenny, television critic, author and columnist for several daily newspapers; Leslie Timmins, head of a centre that trained the clergy in the use of radio and television; and the drama critic and former TV producer Milton Shulman, well known for his strong views on the subject of television and its influence.

Presenter Libby Purves repeated my words and asked me what experience had led me to this view.

'I was brought up entirely without television,' I began. 'In fact, also without electricity . . .' I was interrupted by what seemed to be a genuinely spontaneous roar of laughter from the audience. As far as I could tell, no assistant was holding up a ROAR WITH LAUGHTER board. Perhaps the idea of living without electricity was too fantastic to contemplate in 1982? I waited for the hilarity to subside and gave a brief description of life in the Gloucestershire outback in the 1940s and '50s, with entertainment provided by our wind-up gramophone, all kinds of games and musical instruments, and the wireless with a wet-cell battery that I had to take into the village on my bicycle to be recharged. Then I went on to describe how, after spending much of my early working life in Brazil, I had returned to England in 1975 and become a regular viewer for the first time ever.

'And did you enjoy the television when you had it?' Libby Purves asked.

'Oh yes,' I replied, truthfully. 'Very much, at first. I'd sit and stare at old films and motor racing, but before long I began to feel my TV set was taking me over. My brain would go numb. I felt I was being hypnotised. I would just sit and stare and almost always feel I had completely wasted an evening. That was what really got me. Things were being done to me instead of myself doing things. So one day I decided I wasn't going to live in a brave new world of standardised force-feeding of the mind. I sold the thing.'

'And did you miss it?' Libby Purves asked. 'Did your life deteriorate?'

'Not in the least, no. Immediately – that very day – there was a feeling of exhilaration. There was no cold-turkey period of withdrawal at all.' More laughter. I was becoming a television comedian, it seemed.

I pressed on. 'There was a tremendous joy at rediscovering so many of the pleasures I'd completely forgotten, such

4

as listening to radio, which I hadn't done for a long time.
Since I gave up TV I've become far better informed about
everything, and I'm also better entertained. Not only that,
but I'm much more active because I can listen to concerts
while I'm painting the ceiling.' (This was what I actually
did the day my set went.) I waved my hands in the air
as if wielding a paint roller or conducting an orchestra,
or both, and raised yet another laugh. If the audience
was conditioned to expect constant comedy entertainment,
I thought, let them have it if it makes them more receptive
to the message I was hoping to get across.

'But the main thing,' I concluded, 'is that I have regained
control of my own mind, and that's something I'm not
going to give up again – ever. I've benefited enormously
from my choice and I think others might also benefit if
they watched a great deal less television.'

I had done my best to sound spontaneous, as if I had
made up what I was saying as I went along. In television,
however, things are not always what they seem. My text
had been written out in full, discussed at length and altered
here and there, and then learned by heart. A copy of it was
on the table in front of me, so that I could prompt myself
with an occasional downward glance. It had been made
clear to me that I was expected to stick to my script.

Now it was time for general discussion. Libby Purves
reminded us of some new developments, including cable
and satellite TV networks, a new commercial channel
(Channel 4) and something I preferred not to think about
called Breakfast Television. 'Since it looks as if there's going
to be more of it in Britain,' she said, 'perhaps it is exactly the
time when we should be talking about this. Leslie Timmins,
what do you think?'

'Well, you know,' he began, 'listening to Guy, I really
felt like the two old ladies in Victorian times who prayed
"Please don't let evolution be true, and if it is help us to
hush it up," because the fact is that we are going to have
more. That's not a question, that's a fact. As you said,
Libby, with cable and home video, disc and every manner

of development, we are going to be drenched with more TV.'

Speak for yourself, I thought. I'm not going to have any at all.

'But is this a good thing?' Libby asked. 'Will it rot our brains?'

Leslie Timmins thought not, for two reasons. One was that 'believe it or not, there is a switch called On/Off and any normal human being is entitled to use that switch, and frequently they do.' True – I certainly had, for the last time. The other was that Channel 4 was 'a very serious development' that would provide 'a new opportunity for alternative television'. He ended with the hope that it would be 'quality of programming that should, and I believe will, stand up in the long run, and then we may at least, to use the phrase that Milton made famous, still have "the least worst television in the world".' He was referring to the title of one of Milton Shulman's two books about television. The other, to which I shall be referring later, was *The Ravenous Eye*.

Now it was Shulman's turn. He had been invited as a known anti-TV campaigner, just as Leslie Timmins had been asked to defend the industry with which he had close connections as adviser on religious matters to both the BBC and the Independent Broadcasting Authority. He began by paying me a somewhat surrealist compliment:

'I'd love to stuff Mr Playfair in a bottle,' he said, 'and put him up as Exhibit A for a theory I've had now for at least fifteen years. He substantiates everything I've been saying about television for a very long time. I hate to be a Cassandra about this matter, but it is one of my particular crusades. What you have to realise is that when you talk about being able to switch off, the facts are against you. People *don't* switch off. We now have average viewing figures of something like 3 to 4 hours a day.' This would mean that a person who had watched television from age two to sixty-five, which will become possible early in the twenty-first century, will have spent a total of 10 years in front of a set. (The national average for 1989, according to the BBC's research department, was 3 hours and 46 minutes a day).

'Isn't this broadening our minds and improving us as people?' Libby Purves asked, with a straight face.

Shulman did not think so. He agreed that television could be of some value to the lonely and the sick, and could extend the horizons of the very young through new cultural experiences. 'Unfortunately,' he went on, 'what we have now is a spectator society, a society that's addicted to the box.' A woman who worked in a TV rental shop had told him how some of her customers would react 'like monsters' if their sets broke down and could not be repaired at once. 'What am I going to do?' they would moan. 'I can't be without my TV set for another evening!' One would think, the woman had said, that there was nothing left to live for.

Then there was the survey carried out in Birmingham during a recent television strike that revealed 11 per cent viewing for a blank screen. Shulman produced other statistics that were less amusing: in some areas people went to the cinema once a year, to the opera or ballet one and a half times, and for a walk in the park only three times. Yet when there was a TV strike they would rush to the book-shops and cinemas, bring out the chess and Monopoly sets, and 'most important, talk to their children'. He summed up his case with a brief mention of the subject that makes television people more uncomfortable than any other.

'I would think that in addition to the addiction problem, you have what I do believe is a great contributor to the violence we have in our society, but that's another story.'

'Right, yes, that's another story,' said Libby Purves very quickly. 'Mary, you are a television critic; you in a sense encourage people to watch TV.'

Mary Kenny's soothing Irish tones drove the thought from our minds that there could possibly be a connection between television and violence. She had little to add to the debate, however, and came down half-heartedly on the side of the more-TV lobby. Her main argument was that old favourite, freedom of choice. In the 1990s there would be fifty to sixty channels available, from TV Dubai to TV Alice Springs, and this would lead to a general increase in discrimination, she thought, and be good for us. Then again, home video equipment now made it possible for people to record programmes and watch them in their own time. 'People are using their democratic powers to control TV,' she said, as if this somehow put right everything that might be wrong with it.

Now it was time for the audience to join in our discussion. An anonymous lady in orange immediately drew attention to the most vulnerable of television's victims – children with both parents at work. 'They go back home and it becomes routine to switch on the box,' she said, 'and they therefore become rather minus about it.' A gentleman on the right also expressed concern about the 'garbage' that children were watching. Before this important issue could be discussed further, another man at the back had a polite go at me.

'I find it slightly amusing and rather ironic,' he said, 'that the proposer is using the very medium he is despising so much to put across his case. Is he implying that none of us here in the audience should be sitting here and having our brains rotted?'

Libby Purves beat me to it. 'Mr Gladstone used to consort with prostitutes,' she said sweetly. 'More points? Anyone with Guy Lyon Playfair on this?'

One woman seemed to be. She had been worried for some time about the content of television programmes, and thought there was too much sex and violence. 'But it's something quite new to criticise the actual action of sitting and watching.' This was flattering, but not quite true, as will be shown in due course. She went on to mention a report by the TV Action Group on the effects of television on three- to ten-year-olds. 'They are losing a lot of their culture,' she said. 'They're being discouraged from reading, playing, talking to their parents. Their language is suffering, their perception of reality is suffering, and their general normal development – what we would have considered normal twenty years ago – is suffering. This is something totally new to me and, I think, very interesting.' I also found it interesting and deserving of further discussion.

Next, however, came a somewhat defeatist remark from a man on the left. 'I think there is a telly problem in our present society,' he said, 'but we can't put the clock back. We've got to live with it.' He complained that television went on too late, whereupon somebody reminded him that he could now record late-night programmes and watch them the next day. This was proudly described as 'a new freedom'.

Milton Shulman then made the point that despite all the talk about freedom of choice, the fact was that viewing tastes in Britain were 'solidified in cement', with several of the top ten programmes unchanged for as long as fifteen years. He then suggested that it was possible to break addiction to TV simply by giving it up for one day a month. 'Discover all the glories and excitements,' he said, 'and then you'd break the habit.'

Leslie Timmins, in his summing-up, gave a neat demonstration of a technique often used by politicians in a tight corner – blame somebody else. 'Television, and radio for that matter, is a medium,' he said. 'It isn't an end in itself. What comes out of your screen comes out of the community. It has nowhere else to come from.' If there was anything wrong with television, he seemed to be suggesting, then it is our fault. He ended by noting with approval that 'a lot of things can happen if people take this whole business of choice and selection more seriously.' I could hardly disagree with that.

Libby Purves then asked me for a last word on the way my proposition had been discussed.

'I think it's quite clear that this is a question that should be discussed in far more detail than is possible here,' I said. I would like to have added that there had been no real discussion at all, merely a succession of jump-cuts

9

from one opinion to another. Instead, I pointed out that in Iceland TV was shut down once a week, on Thursdays, and also for the whole month of August. (No longer true, I am sorry to report.) I added that Iceland had the highest standard of living and education in Europe, and wondered if there might be a connection.

The programme came to an end with some desultory comments from members of the audience and an encouraging show of hands which revealed a fair number of 'undecideds' on the question of whether we should have less TV and not more. We then retired to the hospitality room for half an hour or so before being ushered to our taxis and driven our respective ways.

I went home feeling pleased with myself. My proposition had been a straightforward one, and objections to it had been unconvincing. All that hyperbole about our 'democratic powers' and 'new freedom' that enable us to make video recordings or switch channels seemed to me to be symptomatic of the brain-rot to which I had referred, as was the fatalistic assumption that television was here to stay and we just had to put up with it. My suggestion that it was inherently bad for us was one that some people seemed unable to contemplate. Criticising the content of TV programmes was one thing, but attacking the very action of watching anything at all was clearly, as the lady had said, 'something quite new'.

In darker ages, several of my maternal Huguenot ancestors were put to death, most of them buried alive, for attacking the fundamental tenets of the church. Now, instead of suffering the same fate for questioning the whole *raison d'être* of television – which in many respects has assumed the role of a religion – I was treated with courtesy, allowed to say my piece to the viewing public, and even paid £25 for it. If some of my theories on the ways in which television influences people were correct, I had planted a seed of doubt that could be expected to take root here and there.

Although I had been an abstainer for nearly two years,

I decided to watch the transmission on 9 May 1982. Now that I have been identified as an anti-TV campaigner, I thought, I should take a look at it from time to time to remind myself what it is that I am campaigning against. I was glad I did, for I learned something interesting. The programme shown on Sunday was not the one we had recorded on Wednesday. Nearly, but not quite. The editing was skilful and viewers might well have been convinced that they were watching a live spontaneous discussion. Nothing in the *Radio Times* indicated otherwise. Yet it was not live, and while it would be unfair to claim it had been censored, there was no doubt that bits had been cut out. They were not major cuts, and it is only reasonable to expect an editor to remove dull passages from a film, yet the fact remained that viewers were unaware they had been offered a revised reality.

It seemed a trivial point, but it bothered me. Everybody involved in the programme struck me as open-minded and anxious to do an honest professional job. Yet there could be others who were not, and if they held extreme political or religious views they could do a good deal of damage with their discreet revisions of reality. Another programme in which I took part some years later, to be mentioned in due course, proved my fears to be justified.

My début as a TV abolitionist was followed by an article by Milton Shulman in *The Times* under the title 'Imagine Sunday Without TV'.[1] It was hard-hitting stuff, and covered much the same ground as our programme, using some of the same phrases. In a reference to my mention of Iceland's TV-free weekday and month, Shulman thought something similar should be tried in Britain. He suggested the most popular viewing day of the week, Sunday, 'the day of the big fix', and wondered if it was sheer boredom that drove people to their screens 'as administrators in colonial outposts used to be driven to drink'. Why not blank our screens on Sundays and make this the Fun Day of the week? What might happen as a result?

'Millions might find that the family, books, hobbies,

plays, walks in the park, gardening, the cinema were activities more fulfilling than the images on the small screen.' Here was no puritan urging us all to spend Sunday on our knees and spoiling our fun. He wanted us to 'make life fuller, more active, more involved', and he was telling us exactly how this could be done:

Click.

Another, more immediate, consequence of the *Choices* programme was both gratifying and alarming. About three days after the screening, I was listening to a late-night LBC Radio phone-in and not giving it my full attention until the trigger word 'television' made me stop what I was doing, and listen. A woman in south London was calling to say that she had decided to stop watching television, and was explaining why at some length. I was astonished. Hadn't I been saying precisely the same just a few days earlier? The caller made no mention of either me or the *Choices* programme, though she must have seen it, for she was repeating me almost word for word – '. . . felt I was being hypnotised . . . brain going numb . . . standardised force-feeding . . . control of my own mind . . .'

Was I imagining things? Information had been fed into the media system by me, only to re-emerge in a very short time to be fed back into the system, in this case on radio. Was this happening all the time? Could she have absorbed my ideas subliminally and then spontaneously 'thought' them out for herself a few days later? This was not how it sounded. She gave the impression of meaning what she was saying, had already taken the same action as I had, and replied rationally to a couple of questions from the programme presenter. Yet so close was hers to my own expression of distaste that I could not escape the notion I had changed her mind. Can brainwashing be as easy as this?

Of course I was not the first nor even the second person to suggest that there might be something seriously wrong with television – not just with programme content, but with the whole technology. Lee De Forest, one of the fathers of this technology, told the National Association of Broadcasters before he died in 1961 that they had 'debased' his child. 'You have made him a laughing-stock of intelligence,' the angry old man stormed, 'a stench in the nostrils of the gods of the ionosphere.' Milton Shulman, a former Assistant Controller of Programmes for Rediffusion TV, described television in 1973 as 'the Pied Piper leading society nowhere'. Children's writer Marie Winn raised the point that the TV set was a 'pathogen', the source of such symptoms of present-day society's ills as 'alienation, dehumanisation, apathy, moral vacuum'. San Francisco advertising man Jerry Mander was impelled to research and write a long book with the self-explanatory title 'Four Arguments for the *Elimination* of Television', with the word 'elimination' in italics on the title page of the original edition.[2]

Why should these people, and many others, including myself, feel so strongly? My brief statements on the *Choices* programme, carefully scripted and rehearsed as they were, had not told the whole story.

2

MY SECRET SELF

How could I have told the whole story? Television's purpose is not to tell whole stories. It is to entertain, which the dictionary defines as 'to hold the attention, amuse'. The commercial stations have to keep their viewers entertained at all costs in between the advertisements, and the BBC has to compete by providing more of the same. Thus all television becomes entertainment and nothing more.

The best way to hold the viewer's attention, it has been found, is by a succession of rapidly changing images none of which should remain on the screen unaltered for more than a few seconds. Six seconds is, I believe, the generally accepted maximum for everything from chat shows and sports programmes to drama, comedy and of course the daily news. Stories told against this frenzied backdrop of fragmented imagery must be told 'very briefly' or not at all, and the storyteller who feels the need to go into detail is soon brought into line by the phrase, 'What you're saying is . . .', television's euphemism for, 'What we want you to say very briefly'. On one of my first TV appearances, I was asked if I could explain 'very briefly' what something or other was. I replied. 'No. That's why I write books.' I was not invited back to that particular programme. I soon learned that there are strict rules for behaviour on television, as in church or in the presence of royalty.

Even so, my memoirs can be told very briefly indeed insofar as they relate to television. I did not, as I may have implied, go straight from the Cotswolds to Brazil. There was an interval during which my family moved to London and I did my National Service, followed by five years in Cambridge, three gaining a degree and two working for a property developer. The first time I can recall watching anything on television was when I wandered into an empty hut on a bleak RAF station to find the Amadeus Quartet in there playing Mozart, whose music was not improved by all those jittery close-ups of vibrating fingers and shaking heads. On subsequent free evenings I went out in search of live entertainment in the form of the real City of Birmingham Symphony Orchestra or the real Shakespeare company at Stratford-upon-Avon. I was then sent to Iraq, where there was no television at all, so the question of watching it did not arise. I contented myself with playing trombone in the station band, going to the cinema and visiting places like Ur, Babylon and Nineveh at weekends.

Likewise, my memories of life at Cambridge include no trace of television. If there was a set in Pembroke College, I never found it. When not working, I was kept busy playing in the University Jazz Band or pounding an Olivetti portable in my attempts to become a writer – a short story of mine was published in *Granta* after some generous rewriting by editor Michael Frayn, and I was thrilled to see my name on the poster under that of Sylvia Plath. My trombone playing was more successful, as well as more fun, and it led to my screen début in a short film made by an undergraduate named John Tusa, who later rose to some heights in the BBC. It also led to my first appearance on television, in Pete Murray's BBC 'pop' show *Six-Five Special*. Guests, in addition to our band, included an exuberant young fellow named Tommy Steele, and Humphrey Lyttelton and his band. There was also a group of sorts from Oxford, it being Boat Race day, and we were invited to attack each other with soda-water syphons, which we refused to do. Anyway, it was all good fun, and I was mobbed outside the studio by a bunch of groupies who mistook me for Tommy Steele's bass player. I went home feeling that television was not to be taken seriously, a feeling that was to remain unchanged over the years.

There were two good reasons for not acquiring a TV set when I arrived in Rio de Janeiro in 1961: they were expensive luxuries in those days, at least for young teachers, and the evenings were far too hot. Like most Cariocas I would escape the heat and humidity by going to the air-conditioned cinemas as often as possible, and one of the first films I saw was a rather amateurish production called *O quinto poder* (The Fifth Power), which described how a group of neo-Nazis took over the country after a campaign of subliminal propaganda hidden in cinema newsreels. I found it rather implausible and thought no more of it at the time.

Some years later I saw another Brazilian film of considerably more interest. It came on before the main feature and opened with an artistic shot of two nice children in clean clothes playing around in a sunny park until their parents came along, picked up a child each and carried them off – to a discreet and soothing musical soundtrack background. There were no screen titles and nothing was said.

What in the world, I wondered, could this be advertising? Was it a trailer, a documentary, or what? The film came to an end after three or four minutes with a quiet voice murmuring something about 'a new future for a new family'. The following week I saw another of these mysterious commercials for an unknown product, and then another. They were all beautifully photographed, and conveyed an impression of contentment and confidence. They all ended with a single spoken sentence, as had the first one, and it was some time before the unspoken message began to get across.

Life in Brazil at this time was becoming extremely violent. The military had been in power since the 1964 revolution, and after a few years of relative moderation they were becoming very repressive, especially following the kidnapping of the American ambassador and his release in exchange for a group of left-wing political prisoners. There were street riots, during one of which I was tear-gassed at point-blank range. The use of torture by the police became routine, which only made the urban guerrillas more ruthless and determined.

I can never hope to prove that those little mystery commercials had anything to do with the return of social peace, and I can only guess that they were made on the orders of Brazil's intelligence service, the SNI. The military, unlike the characters in *The Fifth Power*, were not trying to take over the country – they had already done that and showed no sign of wanting to give it back to its people. They were nevertheless anxious to win hearts and minds, and having failed to do so by force tried instead indirect suggestion and the soft sell. The films must have been seen several times by every Brazilian of potentially revolutionary age, and in view of what is known about the power of imagery to influence thoughts and actions, it now seems more than likely that the unspoken message was received. *Don't trust those left-wing agitators to improve your lot. Trust us instead.*

It is undeniable that with the appointment of General Emilio Medici as President in the early '70s, things began to calm down. Medici, a moderate and intelligent man compared to his hardline predecessor, was the former head of the SNI, and under his presidency opposition to the military government virtually ceased.

During the fourteen years I spent in Brazil it never occurred to me to buy a television set even when I could afford one. Real life provided all the colour and entertainment I needed. I joined an early music group led by Roberto de Regina, who also taught me to play the harpsichord. I played in the jazz band led by American expatriate Booker Pittman, a former sideman of Count Basie, no less. There was always a film or a play on that was worth seeing, and the Teatro Municipal was visited regularly by the likes of Erroll Garner, Sarah Vaughan and the Modern Jazz Quartet, and on one unforgettable occasion by Igor Stravinsky and the Philharmonia Orchestra. The best popular music in the world was going on, live, all around me, and every year there was the greatest free show on earth – Carnival. Who needed television? If there had been one in my home and I had watched it for 3 hours and 46 minutes every day for fourteen years, I cannot bear to think of all the experiences I would have missed.

As it happens, one of my most memorable experiences of Brazil took place the day before I left it for good, and it was one I would gladly have missed. I was in São Paulo, where I had spent two years researching and writing my first two books, and had just come out of a bank in the city centre when the traffic came to a halt and I heard what sounded like about fifty fire-engines, ambulances and police cars clanging and screaming from all directions. Instinct told me that something awful was happening, as indeed it was.

The following morning, the Mills Brothers were singing *Gently on my Mind* as I collapsed into my seat on the plane at Viracopos Airport. There was nothing gentle on my mind, though. I had not recovered from a nightmare, and that had been nothing compared to what had caused it. Round the corner from my bank a twenty-storey office block was on fire. Flames were coming out of windows about half-way up, leaping with diabolic ferocity. People had rushed to the roof, and in a very short time a helicopter arrived and began to hover at an angle beside the parapet – a very tricky manoeuvre. It could not land on the roof, because of a structure in the middle. I saw people scramble over the parapet and jump into the helicopter. Then, as it began to pull away, another person jumped and missed. At about the same time, others began to fall out of windows, some while trying to climb down knotted sheets to the floor below the fire, others jumping to their death after failing to get either up or downstairs, presumably unable to bear the heat. I saw about ten bodies falling from the front of the building, and knew that many others must be being burned to death inside. All around me, people were crying and praying out loud, crossing themselves and hugging each other for comfort. A big fellow beside me in a smart business suit was sobbing uncontrollably into a silk handkerchief. It was horrible.

It was also great television, I have no doubt, and great entertainment.

Finally calmed by the Mills Brothers and a Varig stewardess, I relaxed and began to look forward to returning to Britain, where people elected their governments and were not brainwashed with subliminal suggestion, or so I thought, and where greedy property developers did not build fire traps. Back in London, I moved into the basement of my brother's house where there was an ancient black and white TV set. All its channels were tuned to a bunch of ghosts lost in a snowstorm, but eventually I managed to get recognisable pictures on the (then) three channels, and at the age of forty I became a regular viewer for the first time in my life.

There were two reasons. I had a set in my room and little else until my belongings came over by sea. Moreover, for the first time ever I felt like withdrawing from my surroundings. Before long, I began to feel *saudades* for the sun, the colour, the cheap mangoes and the general air of exuberant optimism of Brazil. I particularly missed the delightful community spirit of the Japanese quarter of São Paulo, where I had spent the past two years. London was not like that at all. The weather was awful, food and everything else were horrendously expensive, and people were dirty, grey and rude. For a time I even thought of going back to Brazil, where I had felt more at home.

'Crammed into that coffin of an island, you must find wider horizons to express your secret selves,' as Salman Rushdie puts it. I had done that, and I now learned the truth' of his warning to those who emigrate and then return. 'When you have stepped through the looking-glass you step back at your peril. The mirror may cut you to shreds.'[1] Television eased the stepping-back pangs for a time, but disillusionment soon set in. A curious feature of my TV-watching period (1975-80) is that a decade later I could remember very little of what I had seen. Even the films and motor races, which I enjoyed at the time, left none of the memories I had from earlier visits to cinemas and race meetings. It was the news coverage, however, that sowed the first seeds of discontent in my mind.

At that time, the news was often almost exclusively devoted to strikes and industrial disputes, and as I watched the interminable interviews with one manager or union leader after another I noticed that they were all beginning to repeat each other. One day, one of the latter began by declaring, 'My members have not, and nor will we, er . . .' I enjoyed seeing him flounder about in search of a tense that would get him off that syntactical hook, and a few days later a different official was assuring me that his members were not and nor would they. It was as if he had forgotten his lines and remembered somebody else's, rather as the woman mentioned in the previous chapter appeared to have done. The union men all gradually merged into a chorus of now familiar clichés: 'Basically, at this moment in time we've been sold down the river at the end of the day . . .', and so on, while there were always 'technical reasons' for being unable to answer a straightforward question.

True, there were lighter moments. The Prime Minister was lambasted for her 'total lack of ignorance', William Whitelaw accused the Opposition of 'stirring up complacency', and a fellow who had appealed against his conviction for letting his dog make a mess in a park told the cameras, 'I consider I acted in a statesmanlike manner'. Everybody was getting muddled up. It was as though stereotypes had been designed, not only for union leaders but also managers, politicians, sports players – in fact any identifiable group, all members of which felt obliged to conform. Everybody in each group was turning into the same person, as were the TV presenters. They might look different, like a display of ice-cream flavours, but they were all made of the same artificially coloured mixture.

This personality-cloning process even affected groups in which individuality is an essential attribute. I remember watching the actor Robert Mitchum cruising amiably through a chat show, saying some interesting things about his films, and then being put back in his file, as it were, and returned to the vault reserved for film people. He became just another passing image, to be replaced by a bishop, an ex-convict or an acupuncturist. Finally, all these individual images would merge into one and then vanish in the night. To appear on television, I noticed, was to be squeezed dry and discarded.

Paradoxically, while television stripped real celebrities of their status, it also turned people into spurious celebrities. After I had appeared on Thames Television's evening news discussing my fourth book, I was greeted excitedly by one of the counter staff at my bank with, 'Oh, I saw you on telly last night!' She had seen me at least once a week for a couple of years and never mentioned having read anything of mine. Now, after five minutes' chat on the screen, I was somebody famous. Television fame, I learned, meant being famous not for actually having done anything but just for being on television.

This was a trivial matter compared to the way television seemed incapable of providing me with anything except entertainment. The news programmes had their signature tunes, giving them the appearance of soap operas or chat shows, and the newsreaders rather than the news received top billing. The news itself was lost in an endless display of technical trickery. Television, I found, was no more than a kaleidoscope, defined in the American Heritage dictionary as 'a small tube in which patterns of colours are optically produced and viewed for amusement'. In an article I wrote for an environmental magazine even before I had gone TV-free I included this paragraph:

Most serious of all is television's built-in bias away from the general and towards the specific. By focusing the tree at the expense of the forest it promotes superficiality at the expense of depth. In recent times, for example, we have all become familiar with the amiable faces of [steel management and union spokesmen] Sir Charles Villiers and Mr William Sirs, but to understand what the steel strike was really all about we had to listen to [BBC radio news] or read a quality newspaper.[2]

I practised what I had preached by listening to more radio, and finding that politicians and union leaders had plenty to say of interest when given the chance. Television became merely a source of time-filling relaxation.

History began to repeat itself one evening when I was watching Kirk Douglas in the film *Ace in the Hole*. I was wearing wrap-around earphones to keep out the traffic noise. The film ended with a noisy crowd scene in which ambulances, fire engines and police cars converged on the site where somebody has been trapped underground. I was absorbed in the action, my ears filled with sounds of sirens and bells. The film finished and I took off my headphones. To my surprise, I was still hearing sirens and bells. I drew back my thick curtains, and my room began to glow and flicker. The house directly opposite mine was on fire, the top floor blazing fiercely. The whole neighbourhood had turned out to watch as a ladder was shot up to the top floor and a fireman stepped through a window. Tension mounted as he failed to reappear for some time. Then the front door opened and he came out followed by a group of frightened but unhurt people.

'That's what I call public service,' a neighbour commented. We had lived next door to each other for a couple of years, and this was the first time we had exchanged words. Before long the fire was put out, leaving five or six of us having a good gossip and getting to know each other. A pleasant couple invited us all in for a drink, and we had an impromptu party during which I was persuaded to join the local residents' association. Real-life drama had done something for a community that television could never do, and with the emotions associated with the Brazilian office fire still fresh in my mind, I no longer found images of disaster entertaining.

There was another echo from my Brazilian past when

on 1 December 1976 I watched a party political broadcast for the Labour Party made in the form of a cartoon which, in the words of a writer to *The Times* (4 December) made it clear that 'class discrimination is a matter of official socialist policy'. Others went further, describing the film as 'vicious and divisive' and 'deliberately written with a view to stimulating envy, bitterness and class hatred'. The first of these letter-writers was me, and I ended by asking 'Is this kind of irrelevant and illogical nonsense likely to help unite the nation?'

I was reminded of the Brazilian government's soft selling at about the same time of its equally extreme policies. Then I came across a book by Norris McWhirter about his murdered brother Ross, which I read not out of sympathy for their political activities but because I was doing some research into twins and their often claimed ability to communicate by telepathy. There was none of that kind of thing in the book, but there was a chapter headed *A Licence to Brainwash, 1970*. On 8 April of that year, Ross McWhirter thought he had spotted some 'odd flashes' in a party political broadcast (for the Labour Party), and an item in the following morning's *Daily Mail* confirmed his suspicions. According to an unnamed source, there had been three 'subliminal' flashes, images shown so briefly that they could not be consciously assimilated. Subliminal broadcasting was banned in Britain under the 1964 Television Act, and according to the BBC handbook, 'the BBC does not use "subliminal" techniques [that influence viewers without their being] fully aware of what has been done'. Ross McWhirter duly went into action, and armed with an affidavit from the Labour Party mole who had leaked the story, he headed for the Court of Appeal.

The reaction of one of the judges, later to become Lord Chief Justice, was remarkable. He did not find subliminal propaganda all that serious because 'the viewer can always turn it off'. The more perceptive Lord Denning explained that this was precisely what the viewer could not do. 'You can't see it to know when to turn it off.' Even so, he confined his judgment to the hope that it would not happen again, and although the authorities gave assurances that it would not, it was far from clear to me how we would know if it did. If done properly, there would be no complaints to the courts, because nobody would know what had been screened.[3]

One way and another, I was developing a strong allergy to television, and the most frustrating feature of it was that I did not know exactly what was causing my reaction. At the end of an evening's viewing I would feel drained, as if something had been taken from me instead of given to me, as at a concert or a cinema. Fascination would turn to flatness. So much had been promised and so little delivered. It was like having a pain the doctor could not diagnose but that would not go away.

Then, whether by chance or divine guidance, I came across a brief reference to a book already mentioned: Jerry Mander's *Four Arguments for the Elimination of Television*. I wondered at first if he was serious, so I ordered the book from the United States and found that he was, and on 29 August 1980 television went out of my home for good. As I have said, it was much easier than I had thought and there were no withdrawal symptoms at all, but a tremendous feeling of satisfaction that I had repelled an intruder, regained control of my life and my mind, and could now look forward to enjoying real experience again. I celebrated my first TV-free evening by painting my kitchen ceiling to the accompaniment of a Promenade Concert, and the very next day I found all those flickering images of my viewing years had gone away like fragments of a bad dream. Once again I could look for wider horizons.

3

MORE IS LESS

What is wrong with television? There is no single answer to this question, but a great many. All of them are controversial, and none can be discussed 'very briefly', which may explain why none is ever discussed on television. To be sure, there are occasional ritual examinations of the question of television's influence on violent behaviour, but this debate – for which the TV lobby has a standard set of denials, misdirections and obfuscations always at the ready – has diverted attention from other equally important ways in which it affects individuals, families and societies. Indeed, there are those who seem to think that the only argument against television is that it promotes violence. I intend to show how mistaken they are.

There is of course much to be said in favour of television, and its lobby regularly says it. It keeps children quiet as no human baby-sitter can. It consoles the sick, the lonely and the old. It broadens the horizons of just about everybody. It even shapes world events. Was it not TV coverage of the Vietnam war that led to American disillusion and eventual withdrawal? Moreover, the technology has many uses other than home entertainment. Closed circuit TV identifies bank robbers and supermarket thieves, and enables us to look at people before we let them into our homes. Doctors shove tiny TV cameras down our throats and scrutinise our guts at close quarters by endoscopy, now a standard and very efficient diagnostic technique. Ultrasonic scanning also makes use of television with equal efficiency. Patients can even look at their own working parts on the monitor. How can anybody object to such versatile and useful technology that keeps us all safe, well and happy?

People do, though, and they have been objecting very strongly for a number of reasons for at least forty years. How about this for a prediction?

> A race raised on a diet of entertainment shortly will display many of the characteristics of a moron, including the demand for more and more of less and less, and lack of appreciation for services rendered.[1]

That was said in 1949 by – would you believe? – the director of an American television network (Du Mont). At about the same time, Frank Stanton of CBS provoked this blast of protest from Charles Siepmann, one of the earliest objectors to the brave new medium:

> It is indeed the glory of a democratic society that it not merely tolerates but encourages difference, that its concern is with the full flowering of diverse individuality, not of conformity and mass-mindedness. 'Giving the majority of people what they want', which Mr Stanton later dignifies as 'cultural democracy', is that form of tyranny which, as it either excludes or scouts the interests of minorities, is . . . the breeding ground of intolerance and the ultimate death knell of democracy.[2]

The narcotic effect of television was noticed as early as 1948, and the medium was identified as a major and destructive new form of addiction in 1954. In the same year, the first of many large-scale surveys of television and violence was begun, while by 1960 psychologist Hans Eysenck was urging an enquiry into 'the effect which television programmes may have on society generally, including a possible decline in moral standards and the increase in crime among young people'.[3]

As the TV lobby never tires of reminding us, both

the cinema and the radio provoked similar prophecies of doom soon after their arrival. So they did, with some justification in the case of the cinema. Yet each of these media has proved its social and cultural worth, and the criticisms have died down. Criticism of television has not. It has steadily increased, despite opposition from a wealthy and well-trained lobby. Its most determined and influential attackers have included the industry's first major defector, Milton Shulman, American children's writer Marie Winn, the Christian crusader Mary Whitehouse, and even a member of the one industry – advertising – that might be expected to worship the medium and serve it unquestioningly in exchange for huge amounts of money. Yet it was an advertising man, Jerry Mander, who claimed to be the first to raise the idea that television should not be reformed, but got rid of altogether.

Shortly before his book was published in 1978, Mander was telephoned by a TV producer who wanted him to come and talk about it on his chat show, and asked him if he could say in a few words why he wanted to eliminate television. Mander replied that he could not, but needed about a hundred thousand words to explain himself properly. The producer kept trying, as producers always do, and asked what his main points were.

'One of the main points is that television can only deal with main points,' Mander replied, 'so only certain kinds of things can get through.' He then went on to give a sardonic description of how the interview would have gone if he had agreed to do it. There would have been a couple of psychologists and media experts on the show, a lively exchange of views and opinions, 'and in the end the people watching the show wouldn't have learned a damned thing. It would all reduce to who's the better arguer, when the point is really about experience.'[4]

Who is Jerry Mander, and what caused him to take up arms against the sea of television?

Much of his life reads like the traditional American

success story. The son of Jewish immigrants from Eastern Europe, he became upwardly mobile at an early age, deciding that the garment industry was not for him and moving into theatrical publicity and then advertising. By the mid '60s he was a member of the jet set with a prestige San Francisco office and a portfolio of high-profile clients. In a few words, he had made it.

Then doubts began to creep in. He came to realise that advertising's main purpose was to sell people things they did not need, and he became alarmed by the way it allowed him to get into people's heads and, 'like some otherworldly magician, leave images inside that can cause people to do what they might otherwise never have thought to do'.[5]

Turning away from the artificial environment created and sustained by the mass media, he began to take an active interest in the real one. This was in the late '60s, twenty years before green issues became trendy. He pioneered the 'advocacy advertisement' for clients like the Sierra Club and Friends of the Earth, in which the ads not only conveyed information about ecological issues, but included coupons for readers to cut out and send to the appropriate company or public authority. Not surprisingly, he began to lose his prestige clients, and in 1972 he disbanded his agency and set up America's first non-profit public relations and advertising firm devoted exclusively to promoting community and ecological causes. This did well for a time, but Mander began to feel he was 'throwing snowballs at tanks' as every small victory was followed by a dozen new crises. Even more disturbing than the unchecked advance of environment-unfriendly 'progress' was an alarming new trend in the way people were becoming unwilling to think coherently about things that affected their lives. The information explosion had become a glut, leading not to involvement but to passivity.

Then, Mander recalls, he came across some 'amazing' statistics. The most amazing statistic I ever saw, in a Brazilian newspaper famous for its misprints, announced that 103 per cent of Brazilians ate too much sugar. Even in the early '70s, the figures for TV ownership and daily viewing were almost as amazing: 99 per cent of Americans had access to a set and they stared at it for six hours a day, eight if they were children. Direct experience of almost everything except sleep and work was a thing of the past. The medium had become the Great Mediator.

Information was being standardised as well as mediated, with up to thirty million people on any given evening being fed the same 'experience'. Viewers were finding it difficult to distinguish between real-life experience and what was being processed, packaged and shoved at them down the tube. The most insidious part of the whole process was the 'new muddiness of mind' brought about by TV-watching that kept people unaware of what was being done to them.

The extent of television's influence had become evident by 1960, when John F. Kennedy won the closest presidential election in US history, beating Richard M. Nixon by just over 100,000 votes out of the 64 million cast. It was generally accepted at the time that the famous TV debates between the candidates tipped the balance in Kennedy's favour. Four hours on the screen were more effective than months of speeches up and down the country. Nixon learned his lesson, cleaned up his TV act and won in 1968 by 0.7 per cent of the vote. From then on, politicians had to be media-smart to get anywhere, and Mander noted that the Carter-Reagan contest of 1976 was something of a first in that it displayed 'no content at all, only form', and was reduced to 'a contest between images and advertising stereotypes'.

Not only presidential candidates were catching on fast. Minority interests were no longer being 'scouted', as Siepmann put it (meaning derided or scoffed at). They had cottoned on to what Mander identifies as the 'hierarchy of press-oriented actions'. This begins with a press conference, which tends to be rather boring television. A march is better, and a sit-in better still. Best of all is some violence. The hierarchy was being extended to its logical limits as kidnappers, hijackers and bombers were admitting that their main objective was getting to say their piece on television. So in addition to mediating and standardising information, television was actually making things happen.

Mander's four arguments for the elimination (not reform) of television can be summarised in the traditional TV manner – very briefly:

1. Television mediates and confines experience, creating an artificial environment in which the viewer has no direct contact with the real world.

2. Television controls and colonises experience. It gives the few the chance to control the many. It offers millions the same indirect experience. It promotes passivity, discourages self-reliance, and separates individuals from each other and from society. It reshapes people to fit the environment it has invented.

3. Television does both mental and physical harm. It induces something very similar to a hypnotic trance. The fluorescent light it emits directly affects our bodies. It is highly addictive.

4. Television contains built-in biases that determine what it can convey, and so is essentially anti-democratic.

Mander concludes, after presenting a mass of evidence in support of each argument, that television is 'a totally horrible technology' and that reforming it is out of the question. 'Its problems are inherent in the technology itself to the same extent that violence is inherent in guns.' It has to go.

Strong stuff. Could he be overstating his case? Was it valid in Britain, where by general agreement we have the best (or as Shulman puts it 'the least worst') television in the world? Did it apply to non-commercial television? I put these points to him, and he agreed that the overall quality of the British product was better than almost anything the United States could offer, and the lack of commercial interference on the BBC was a good thing.

Yet, when you take into account all of the effects of television – the organizing principles of such a centralized medium, the political effects thereof, the concentration of information within such a narrow-band information channel (as compared with print, radio and life!), the replacement of direct experience by a surrogate second-hand life, the inevitable distortions of content which nonetheless pass for reality, the confusions between the real and the not-real, the varieties of other psychological and biological effects which are intrinsic to heavy viewing, the control of information in a few hands, the passiveness which contributes towards an eventual autocratic arrangement, the encouragement of techno-dazzle, the breakdowns in family life and neighborhood life, the isolation, the increasing hard-edgedness of the information we experience, the one-dimensionality of knowledge, the tendency toward unification of mind, the suppression of environmental understanding, the speeding-up of the human perceptual framework, and the alienation from natural rhythm, to name just a few applicable effects to any culture which is thoroughly wired-in and viewing heavily as England is – then I would say that the great majority of the hundreds of the effects described in the book ought to be thought applicable to England. (What a sentence that was!)[6]

It was indeed, and it emphasised the point that it is not so much the content of TV programmes that affects us as the mere act of watching. This is a feature of the debate that is seldom discussed in any detail, which is hardly surprising. Where would it be discussed? Not on BBC radio, which depends on TV licence fees. Not on commercial radio, where with one or two exceptions nothing is discussed at all except politics, sport and pop music. Not by television critics with their vested interest in the medium. Not, obviously, on television. Even in books and articles in scientific journals, where we might expect detailed discussion, attention is almost exclusively devoted to programme content and violence.

The first major anti-television campaigner was Milton

Shulman, who fired a devastating broadside against it in his well-documented 1973 book in which he identified it as the 'fifth factor' at work in the shaping of young minds, the other four being the only factors that influenced children's development throughout history until the 1950s: the home, the neighbourhood, the school and the church. Having spent six years in the business himself, he knew what he was talking about. Yet rather than blowing television out of the water, he had concluded with a call for a National Broadcasting Council to find ways of raising standards.[7] This seems to me like asking St George to domesticate the dragon instead of running his sword through it.

The second crusader of the 1970s was American author Marie Winn, whose horrifying study of the effects of TV on American children first appeared in 1977. She was probably the first to explain in detail why the effect of watching anything at all on television was just as influential as programme content, and she did more than anybody else to open the eyes of parents to the fact that a new generation was being telly-weaned to such an extent that it was quite unprepared for normal life. She supported her case with a mass of first-hand testimony from parents, teachers and children, and took the trouble to find and interview a number of families who had taken the plunge and gone TV-free. Yet Winn is not an abolitionist. Her aim, she says, is not to make television go away but to promote a new way of thinking about it.[8]

Undoubtedly the critic to make the most impact in Britain is Mary Whitehouse, a moral crusader in the tradition of Christian militancy who deserves credit for getting her message across to those who most need to hear it, and for refusing to give up. However, she and her fellow-members of the National Viewers' and Listeners' Association are by definition consumers who want to clean up the media and not get rid of them.

Jerry Mander did not abolish television overnight, though he did at least draw his sword and have a go at the beast. His book sold 60,000 copies in its first two years, and found its way into the syllabuses of several university departments, thereby spreading the idea that TV should and could be eliminated if only by individuals. To start a grass-roots movement one has to scatter the seeds and wait for nature to do the rest.

In 1982, when I took my pot-shot at the dragon on *Choices*, there was no fourth channel in Britain, no breakfast television, no all-night programming every night of the week, no cable and no satellite broadcasting. By the end of the decade the dragon had spawned quintuplets, for all of these had either arrived or were on the way. Viewers were also facing the prospect of buying expensive new sets in order to enjoy High Definition TV – the 1250-line MAC (multiplexed analogue components) system in Europe and MUSE (multiple subnyquist sampling encoding) for Japan and the USA. By the time all that was obsolete, there would be three-dimensional or stereoscopic TV in the home, perhaps even wall-to-wall (plus floor and ceiling) 'multi-viewpoint holography' which would in effect turn an entire room into a replacement for the old-fashioned screen.[9]

Television, by 1990, was on the rampage, trampling across every area of national life and devouring whatever it could get its jaws into. It had battered its way into the House of Commons and the courts of law, reminding us who was really running the country. It had long ago downgraded the Queen to just another image the same size as all the others, while the heir to the throne had become just another TV presenter. Yet television still had plans for us. Where would it all end?

When I rid my home of television in 1980, I was more interested in my own future well-being than that of the nation. I wanted to see if I would be better off without it, and, having soon found that I was, decided to stay without it. Then I began to look at it – or rather not to look at it – in a new way, as I came to realise that there was rather more to the anti-television case than any of my predecessors had indicated, and that it should be told.

I found I had already done relevant research for my book on hypnosis in such areas as direct and indirect suggestion, subliminal communication, and mind-manipulating techniques of many kinds. I also felt uniquely qualified to present the whole case, being the first, as far as I knew, to write on the subject as a non-viewer. Moreover, I was one of the few survivors of a vanishing breed – those who grew up entirely without television. This gave me what the lawyers call *locus standi*, or status.

PART TWO

With the development of television . . .
private life came to an end.

That was the ultimate subtlety: consciously to
induce unconsciousness, and then, once
again, to become unconscious of the act of
hypnosis you had just performed.

George Orwell, *Nineteen Eighty-Four*

4
OPIUM OF THE PEOPLE

Sight is our dominant sense. It is a versatile one, able to take in a wide range of information at the same time and to interpret it either as a sequence of individual items (tree, dog, lawn, sky) or as a whole (view from window). It is also relentlessly demanding. We can go a long time without any of the other senses providing us with more than the minimum of input, but our eyes demand to be fed as insistently as a hungry infant. Moreover, they demand it all the time. Even when we are asleep we have to fill the void with our dreams.

They are not satisfied with any old nourishment, however. They need something new, and preferably moving. On train journeys, we look up from our books or newspapers to stare out of the window rather as we might take a sip of water during a lecture. If there is no refreshing image to be seen, we go back to our reading in search of the artificial images created by our imagination. To remain active, our brains need images as much as our bodies need air and water.

Babies are born with some experience of all their senses except that of sight, and from the moment they open their eyes it is visual information that claims priority for their attention. They explore their new environment in every way they can, touching and tasting everything within reach, and registering sounds and smells. Yet give a baby something to look at and it will look at it. If it is new and interesting and moves about, the baby will go on looking at it indefinitely. Television might have been invented to satisfy this instinctive need.

There is even evidence that some babies are born addicted to television. This extraordinary suggestion was put forward in 1988 by psychologist Dr Peter Hepper of Queen's University of Belfast after he had carried out a simple and highly original experiment with fifteen babies four to five days after their birth. He divided them into two groups, the control group and the 'soap' group. All the mothers of the seven babies in the latter group were regular viewers of the TV soap opera *Neighbours*, while the mothers of the eight control babies were not. Dr Hepper then played the programme's theme music to all the babies individually and noted their reactions. Six out of the seven 'soap' babies went into the 'quiet alert state' as soon as they heard the music, while only two of the eight control babies did so. The two babies in the soap group who were crying before the music started immediately stopped, whereas the four crying babies in the control group went on crying.

Dr Hepper pointed out that there was good evidence from other sources indicating that sound signals can be perceived and learned by unborn babies, especially sounds associated with their mothers' relaxed states during pregnancy. He noted that viewers of *Neighbours* mentioned 'settling down with a cup of tea' or 'putting their feet up' while watching it and so were clearly relaxed. This offered an ideal setting for the 'conditioning' brought on by regular exposure, and whether seriously or not he used the phrase 'fetal addiction' to describe the result.[1]

In view of this prenatal conditioning, it is hardly surprising that babies soon accept the television set, with its unlimited supply of novelties in the form of moving images, as a normal part of the environment. We instinctively give priority to visual stimuli as soon as we open our eyes, and these continue to dominate throughout our lives. We can only come to terms with our environment – cave, house or office – if we automatically absorb any new information that might affect it, and therefore us. In ancient times this had considerable survival value. If something stirred in the forest it could be a predator about to attack us or a prey that we could hunt for dinner. We might have been originally alerted by a sound, but we could only classify the intruder as food or foe by having a look at it.

Another reason for the dominance of the visual sense is that it can reach further than any other. We can see most things long before we can hear them, we cannot smell them until they are fairly close, and we can only taste and touch by direct contact. So sight is our early-warning radar system, and like any other kind of radar it must always be on the alert, scanning its whole field of vision. This applies whether we are making our way through the Amazon forest or across the Cromwell Road, and it means that we will always take in far more information by sight than by any other sense.

For all its variety, the natural imagery we see around us is not enough – we fill our homes with pictures and ornaments, we read books in search of mental images, and we now add to this plethora with permanent and continuous visual stimulus from the television machine, which is first and foremost an image-maker. Some go so far as to 'devote or give (themselves) habitually or compulsively' to it, thus becoming addicts, as defined by the American Heritage dictionary, which goes on to say that the word is used especially with regard to a narcotic. This in turn is usually taken to mean some kind of drug, but according to the same dictionary it also means 'something that numbs, soothes or induces a dreamlike or insensitive state'. That sounds to me like rather a good description of television.

Its sedative qualities were noticed as soon as the first members of the telly generation (children brought up with TV in the home) were born. 'With the tots fanned out on the floor in front of the receiver', a critic wrote in 1948, 'a strange if wonderful quiet seems at hand.' Children's viewing was, he added, 'an insidious narcotic' – not for the kids but for their parents, who were now guaranteed peace and quiet for themselves by administering the tele-sedative to the tots. 'Surely', Marie Winn comments, 'there can be no more insidious a drug than one you must administer to others in order to achieve an effect for yourself?'[2]

That it was having an effect on children as well was recognised as early as 1954 when an article appeared in a medical journal with the uncompromising title 'Television addiction and reactive apathy'. The author was Dr Joost Meerloo, an associate professor at the New York School of Psychiatry who had served during World War II as chief of psychological warfare in the Netherlands government and so presumably knew a thing or two about how to influence minds. 'Although it is a well-known fact', he began, 'that television has a hypnotic and seductive action on its audience, not very much has been said concerning the alarming pathogenic action of this dream factory on special types of onlookers.' The previous year he had seen three adolescent patients suffering from 'increasing mental apathy' who 'apart from their television interest showed a general apathy towards everything'. From these three case studies, Meerloo was able to reach the following conclusions:

1. Television fascination is a real addiction, that is to say, television can become a habit-forming device, the influence of which cannot be stopped without active therapeutic interference.
2. It arouses precociously sexual and emotional turmoil, seducing children to peep again and again, though at the same time they are confused about what they see.
3. It continuously provides satisfaction for aggressive fantasies (midwestern scenes, crime scenes) with subsequent guilt feelings – since the child unconsciously tends to identify with the criminal, despite all the heroic avengers.
4. It is a stealer of time.
5. Preoccupation with television prevents active inner creativity – children and adults merely sit and watch

the pseudoworld of the screen instead of confronting their own difficulties. If there is a conflict with the parents – who have no time for their youngsters – the children surrender all the more willingly to the screen. The screen talks to them, plays with them, takes them into a world of magic fantasies. For them, television takes the place of a grown-up, and is forever patient. This the child translates into love.

It is remarkable to see how many of the problems caused by television were so clearly identified at a time when a set was an expensive luxury owned by less than half the population of the United States. Meerloo even anticipated some of Mander's arguments mentioned in the previous chapter:

> We must keep in mind that every step in personal growth needs isolation, needs inner conversation and deliberation, and a reviewing with the self. Television hampers this process and prepares the mind more easily for collectivization and cliché thinking. It persuades onlookers to think in mass-values. It intrudes into family life and cuts off the more subtle interfamilial communication.[3]

Meerloo may have reached these conclusions after a study of only three patients, all of whom might well have been in a mess even if there had been no TV set in their homes. Yet we should not assume that they apply only to the emotionally disturbed. As will become apparent, some of them were to be equally applicable more than thirty years later, and applicable to everybody.

This is especially true of his identification of 'a real addiction' from which millions now suffer, and it needs repeating because few seem to be aware of it and even fewer have even considered that they might be better off if they gave it up, as they would be if they kicked any other addictive habit. Massive campaigns have been mounted against alcohol, tobacco, heroin and cocaine, yet the idea that addicts should do something about their television habit is almost never heard.

There are several reasons why this is so. Television is universally accepted as a normal part of modern family life, even as one without which normal life would be impossible. Then there is an enormously wealthy and powerful lobby acting on its behalf, supported by the popular press. Sociologists Laurie Taylor and Bob Mullan discovered in the course of their 1986 survey that the tabloids employed no less than forty full-time television reporters; a sampling of five daily and five Sunday papers during a single week produced a total of 174 items related to television. The popular press, they found, devoted considerably more space to television news and gossip than to foreign affairs.[4]

A third reason is that some of the effects caused by TV addiction are subtle and indirect. It does its damage while persuading addicts that they are enjoying nothing more than what Taylor and Mullan describe as 'mild distractions, gentle pleasures and sheer delights'. Thus television covers its own tracks.[5] Even so, there are those who are well aware of what is going on. Jerry Mander has compiled a collection of some two thousand comments made to him about television in letters and conversations and has made a short list of those most often repeated. Examples:

'I feel hypnotised when I watch television.'
'I feel like it's brainwashing me.'
'I feel like a vegetable when I'm stuck there at the tube.'

People also said that television was taking over their brains, turning their minds to mush or destroying them altogether, sucking energy and generally making them stupid. One respondent stated simply that 'television is an addiction and I'm an addict'. Mander's small son came out with a fairly shrewd remark one day when he complained that he didn't want to watch as much TV as he did, but he couldn't help it – 'It makes me watch it'.

Mander recalls his own regular viewing days in words that express perfectly my own feelings from mine. Even after watching a programme on a subject of special interest to him, he would feel that the experience of watching it had been 'antilife' and had left him feeling 'drained in some way' or just 'used'. He described feeling 'a kind of internal deadening, as if my whole physical being had gone dormant, the victim of a vague soft assault'. Can there be a better description of a narcotic at work?[6]

Taylor and Mullan collected some interesting testimony in this context during the course of their generally favourable survey of viewers' opinions. A mother in her thirties admitted that her children's lives and her own were 'controlled by the telly'. Another woman confessed to feeling ashamed and embarrassed by her viewing habit and felt she should be 'doing more with my time and my life'. A man described television in his home as 'a permanent thing', explaining that 'if you turn the light on you might as well turn the TV on . . . might as well be on the same switch, really'. Some even admitted leaving their sets switched on virtually all the time whether anybody was watching them or not. One woman felt 'very cold' when hers was off and felt 'it should be on'. Another commented: 'I'm not watching telly all the time, it's just there and it's on.'[7]

This is a peculiarity not often found in other addictions. Alcoholics, for instance, do not pour themselves drinks and then leave them to evaporate, at least not on purpose. Yet television addicts apparently feel better if their sets are entertaining the empty air while they are out. Part of television's extraordinary hold on domestic life may have something to do with the passing of the open fire from most urban homes. The fireside was the traditional centre of off-duty family life for centuries, and many still derive pleasure from doing no more than staring at flickering flames. Presumably this is why both the gas and electricity industries make their own imitations of the real thing. We would not think of putting out a real fire every time we left the room, so why switch off the TV?

It may be that television serves to fulfil a powerful need that has been bred into us since the days of gathering round the cave fire for both warmth and mutual support. It has replaced the open hearth as the focal point of family life, yet there is an important difference between an open fire and a TV set, apart from their obviously different functions. The fire has no information content and provides no images other than the flickering of flames, a warm glow in the room and the occasional shifting of a log. It is an ideal focus for inducing a meditative state, one in which the mind can rest from the business of absorbing new images and sort out those received earlier in the day.

Such states of reverie can be more than merely relaxing. In 1865, the chemist Friedrich von Kekulé sat by his fire and made a major breakthrough in the history of organic chemistry, seeing with his 'mental eye' the solution to a problem that had been bothering him for some time – the structure of certain molecules of organic compounds. It was probably not a daydream but a hypnagogic image, one of those brief flashes of vivid imagery that many people experience just as they are dropping off to sleep and immediately forget. Two features of Kekulé's famous description of his vision are particularly interesting: he saw it, in his words, after 'I turned my chair to the fire and dozed,' and although he does not tell us if he gazed into the flames before dozing, it is difficult to turn one's chair towards a fire without doing this. He then explains that it was 'my mental eye, now rendered more acute by repeated visions of this kind' that enabled him to interpret the image correctly. When he concluded his account by saying 'Let us learn to dream, gentlemen!' he meant what he said.[8]

One does not make major breakthroughs just by staring at fires, of course. The groundwork has to be done first. If I was shown the cure for the common cold, AIDS or whatever, I would not have the faintest idea what it was and I would almost certainly forget it anyway. Having done quite a bit of work sharpening my own mental vision and learning to dream, I can recognise flashes of imagery that relate to my own work or problems, and I know that problems have a way of solving themselves if I feed them into the mind, leave them alone and go off and do something else. Yet solutions will only pop out when the conscious mind is in neutral. There was a cartoon some years ago in an American business magazine showing an employee complaining about a colleague who had been given a raise although he spent most of his time staring out of the window. 'If you saw what he sees when he stares out of windows, I'd give you a raise too,' was the boss's reply.

Now, suppose Kekulé had been watching television after a hard day in the lab instead of sitting by his fire. The history of organic chemistry might have taken a different course. To be sure, he might have solved the benzene ring molecule problem later. Or he might not. If today's scientists were to put in half an hour at the fireside when they got home, instead of slumping in front of a soap opera, who can tell how many problems might be solved sooner rather than later, or not at all?

The mere act of watching television, whatever the programme, fills the head with new imagery and so interferes with its task of processing the imagery already there. Suggestions that heavy viewing turns the mind to mush may not be far from the truth. It not only drives the brain waves into patterns that make organised thought impossible, but it leaves the poor overloaded brain with simply no time to handle the mail, as it were, before the next lot comes crashing through the box. Fire-gazing has an entirely opposite effect: it brings families together and gives its members the chance to sort the day's information intake both consciously and unconsciously. Television, on the other hand, brings families together in the way that sheepdogs bring sheep together, herding them from one image sequence to the next and making sure that viewers of the nationwide flock cannot stray off to do their own thing. The television set does indeed make you watch it, and it knows it. Like your friendly neighbourhood dope pedlar, it knows you will be back for more.

Marie Winn has listed the essential features of addiction (to anything) and shown how directly each of them relates to television:

1. The pursuit of pleasure.
2. The search for a 'high' that normal life does not supply.
3. The increasing inability to function normally without the substance in question.
4. The need for indefinite repetition of the dose.
5. The loss of discrimination brought about by excessive intake.
6. The narrowing and dehumanising of life caused by the above.

There is nothing wrong with the pursuit of pleasure, of course, and such a pursuit need not be addictive. It only develops into real addiction when the victim becomes dependent on it and cannot get satisfaction from anything else. In the process it becomes less and less enjoyable and more and more necessary, eventually becoming the only necessity and taking complete control of the addict's life.

'The testimonies of ex-television addicts often have the evangelical overtones of stories heard at Alcoholics Anonymous meetings,' says Marie Winn, who collected a good deal of such testimony at first hand. One reformed addict recalled how his mind had been 'completely mummified' throughout his viewing years. 'I was glued to that machine and couldn't get loose, somehow.' He and his wife would watch TV all evening, every evening, whether the programme was good, bad or indifferent. He would feel angry with himself for wasting so much time and not doing the things he really wanted to do such as labelling his slide collection and reading all the back issues of the magazines that had been piling up unread – 'I only had time for television'. When the set broke down one day, he snapped out of his prolonged trance and decided to see what would happen if he did not have the set repaired.

That, he said, was the smartest thing he ever did. 'I can hardly believe we could have lived like that,' he said later.

Others still did live like that. A lawyer admitted to watching television 'the way an alcoholic drinks'. He would watch 'any programme at all' even if it did not appeal to him. He admitted to being an addict, and to being unhappy about his addiction, yet he insisted there was nothing he could do about it. 'I'll sit there getting madder and madder at myself for watching, but still I'll sit there. I can't turn it off.'

This miserable confession does not sound to me much like the pursuit of 'mild distractions, gentle pleasures and sheer delights' described by Taylor and Mullan. Nor do Winn's appalling descriptions of the behaviour of addicted children like the ten-year-old child described by his mother as 'hooked on TV as an alcoholic is hooked on drink', or the eight-year-old who went through 'withdrawal symptoms' when the family set broke down, becoming fidgety and nervous as if not knowing what to do with himself to the point where 'I felt that if he didn't watch something he was really going to start climbing the walls'.[9]

Horror stories of which these are just a small sample make it clear that television addiction can be as debilitating and degrading as any other. The saddest aspect of it is the sheer pointlessness of it all. We do not hear people expressing guilt and frustration about their reading, theatre- or even cinema-going habits. Stamp collectors do not beat their breasts in despair for the time they waste poring over their treasures. People take their cars to bits without lamenting all those lost weekends. Gardeners are not to be found mesmerised by their roses and wishing they could drag themselves indoors to watch something.

The television addict is a pathetic creature who deserves sympathy, yet this is the one addiction we prefer not to acknowledge. Alcohol consumption is regulated by huge taxation and strict licensing hours. Tobacco consumers are also highly taxed and are forced to abstain in an increasing number of public areas. Chemicals that can be addictive are controlled by the requirement for a prescription or banned altogether. Only TV addiction goes untreated and unregulated.

For the price of a colour TV licence, an alcoholic can keep going for a couple of weeks, a heavy tobacco user for perhaps a month, and a heroin or cocaine consumer only about a day. The TV addict has an unlimited supply, twenty-four hours a day, every day for a whole year. Thus of all known addictions this is by far the cheapest, so it is not surprising that it is also the most widespread. To children it is of course free.

Pearl Coleman, who runs an alternative medicine clinic in Woking, points out that television and not religion is what Marx called 'the opium of the people' and thinks it is time general practitioners prescribed less of it for their patients. 'Accepting that the "box" could be described as a hypnotic, sedative, tranquilliser, stimulant, etc, should not the same concern be given to overdosing with it as to the pill form causing such effects?' she asks. Among the mental and physical effects she reckons to be TV-related are myopia, obesity, malnutrition, speech disorders and anti-social behaviour especially of the violent kind. She has even noticed some effects on herself after one of her rare evenings of 'run of the mill' viewing: 'I confess to having at the end of it nothing less than a sense of deprivation and time-wasting which has made me thoroughly irritable.'[10]

Admitting that one has a problem is the first step towards overcoming it, and many TV addicts do admit this. Others seem to take the attitude of the musician Charlie Parker who, a couple of hours before his death, aged thirty-four, from the combined effects of alcohol and heroin, told a doctor that 'I enjoy a sherry before dinner.'

The good news for the TV addict is that giving up can be surprisingly easy. Unlike almost all other narcotics, television can be replaced at once by something more satisfying and less harmful. Everything that is provided by television is also available from other sources. Therefore in giving it up one is not really giving anything up altogether except the act of staring at a small screen, and who really needs to do that?

5

CONFUSED?

We all take in far more visual information than we need, and we keep all of it whether it seems useful or not. In fact, we cannot get rid of it even if we would like to do so. True, we forget things, but this is due to retrieval malfunction rather than actual loss of an item in the memory store. Indeed, to get rid of traumas, those emotional shocks usually from childhood that affect mental stability later in life, prolonged psychiatric treatment may be necessary. Our natural instinct is to register whatever information the environment throws at us, process what we need at the time and tuck the rest away, just as we fill our attics with things that will 'come in useful one day'. There is no known limit to the storage capacity of our memory attics.

The brain, however, can become overloaded during the information-collecting process, and when this happens it resorts to a rather curious defence mechanism. Here is an example of information overloading:

Your right arm is becoming heavier. At the same time your left arm feels lighter and the right foot feels numb. Now your right arm feels lighter still while the left is becoming heavier and begins to fall. The left hand is also feeling numb and cold. At the same time you notice how warm your left foot is getting, while your right arm is becoming so heavy that you cannot lift it without considerable effort. All the while, your left hand continues to feel warmer and warmer and as it does so it gets lighter and lighter and begins to lift into the air.

Confused? You should be, because this piece of apparent nonsense from one of the standard textbooks on medical hypnotism illustrates what is known in the trade as the Confusion Technique, used to induce hypnosis in difficult subjects. If contradictory and thoroughly confusing statements like the above are made for five or ten minutes, this is what should happen next: 'The effort of trying to adopt a critical attitude towards all of the conflicting suggestions proves too much, so that eventually the line of least resistance is adopted and criticism is suspended.' The patient is then 'resigned to accepting the suggestion which is really desired'.[1] Desired by the hypnotist, that is.

Our brains also react in a predictable way when they are confronted not by too much information but by too little. Here is hypnotist, James Braid, describing the conclusion he reached after numerous experiments on his patients:

> It is a law in the animal economy that by a continued fixation of the mental and visual eye on any object which is not of itself of an exciting nature, with absolute repose of body and general quietude, they become wearied; and provided the patients rather favour than resist the feeling of stupor of which they will soon experience the tendency to creep upon them during such experiments, a state of somnolency is induced . . . which renders the patient liable to be affected . . . so as to exhibit the hypnotic phenomena.[2]

Braid, writing in 1843, had rediscovered what eastern meditators had known for centuries: concentration on a single object can lead to an altered state of consciousness. His important discovery was that this state could be used together with spoken suggestion to help the sick get better, and so medical hypnotism as still practised today evolved from mesmerism with its unspoken indirect suggestion (which could be just as effective). Braid found that any object would do provided patients kept their eyes fixed on it. Bright ones were best, and he normally used his shiny metal lancet-case held in front of the patient's eyes. 'The patient must be made to understand', he wrote, 'that he is to keep the eyes steadily fixed on the object, and the mind riveted on the idea of that one object.'[3]

Now, what do we do when we watch television? We fix our eyes on a not very exciting object as we slump in absolute repose. We definitely favour the feeling that creeps upon us, so much so that we go favouring it indefinitely or until the weather forecast reminds us that it is bedtime. All the while we are being submitted to prolonged application of Confusion Technique (in the modern form of what Mander calls 'techno-dazzle') with images hurtling at us one after the other at a rate of at least ten a minute, hour after hour. While watching television we are thus hypnotised in two ways at once.

Being hypnotised does not, as some believe, mean that we are out cold. Even in the deepest of trances information reaches the mind, while in light hypnosis we remain fully aware of everything around us. So the images absorbed by the television viewer, though they may be consciously forgotten (as they often are) will remain in the memory store. What they do with themselves in there and when they will pop out into consciousness, sometimes altering behaviour in the process, is entirely beyond our conscious control.

At the 1988 conference of the Market Research Society, Roy Langmaid and Wendy Gordon provided evidence to suggest the existence of something called Shoppers' Trance. They tested a group of volunteer supermarket shoppers for 'brand awareness' (buying one item in preference to a similar one made by another company) and then hypnotised them and gave them the same test. The researchers found that brand awareness was considerably better under hypnosis, and they also reported that from their own observations they reckoned 'lots of people shop in trance', largely as a result of the relaxation induced by Muzak. 'Could it be', they asked, 'that in the absent-minded trance-like state which we observed in the supermarket aisles, people replay snippets of the commercials, the branding and atmosphere they experience at home in a similar state while glued to the box, swaying rhythmically while doing the ironing, feeding the cat or cooking the evening meal?'[4]

I am not sure that Shoppers' Trance works quite like this (do people sway while feeding the cat, or cooking?), but this is an example of the kind of first-hand research of which there should be a good deal more. It seems to provide clear evidence that people buy things for reasons they cannot explain, and if they do that what else might they be doing without knowing why?

Another example of a very under-researched aspect of television is the experimental study of viewers' brain waves carried out by biofeedback specialist Thomas Mulholland in the early '70s. Even if it is an exaggeration to say that watching TV turns the brain to mush, we certainly know now that it does alter brain functioning quite dramatically. Mulholland discovered this when he wired ten young people to electroencephalograph (EEG) machines and sat them down in front of TV sets to watch one of their favourite programmes. He expected to see plenty of fast beta wave activity (13 to 50 cycles per second) on the EEG, indicating that his subjects were actively responding to something they enjoyed. Instead, all he could see on the paper were the slower alpha waves (about 7 to 13 cycles per second) of the kind associated with relaxation, meditation and other wholly passive states in which the subject is not interacting with the outside world at all.

Mulholland then fixed his apparatus so that the TV sets would switch themselves off automatically when the EEG showed a predominance of alpha. In other words, if the children did not generate any higher (beta) waves of the kind produced during conversation or reading, in which the speaker or reader is actively interacting with the other speaker or the book, the switching off of the set would prove that the children had not been interacting with the imagery. Mulholland found that while most children learned with practice to keep their sets on, they were not very good at it to begin with; only one or two could keep them on for more than half a minute at a time.

'Viewing TV is rather odd in terms of attention,' Mulholland concluded. 'Children watching TV often drop to a rather low level of arousal, with plenty of alpha.' This, he said, led him to speculate that 'children may be spending a huge amount of time learning how to be inattentive.' Home television viewing was in effect conditioning them to 'operate at a low level of attention'. He wondered how this might be affecting their school performance. 'More research is surely indicated here, since children spend a huge amount of time watching TV before they start school.'[5]

More research into TV and brain waves was in fact being done at about the same time by Herbert Krugman, manager of corporate public opinion research at General Electric. He was interested in comparing the ways in which people respond to print and imagery, and his findings fully supported those mentioned above. He took his subject, a twenty-two-year-old secretary, into a specially prepared room in the Neuropsychological Laboratory of New York Medical School, and told her to make herself comfortable, relax and look at the magazines provided. From time to time the TV set in the corner would show a series of three contrasting commercials, repeating them a few times. Two were quiet, low-key advertisements – one for a heart pacemaker, the other for a hair conditioner – while the third was a 'very explosive' one in which a baseball star hurled balls at a sheet of unbreakable artificial glass.

Wired to the EEG, the woman browsed through the magazines for a quarter of an hour, showing special interest in an advertisement for Max Factor make-up. Her brain-wave ratio at this point was 5:16:28 – that is, five seconds of slow waves in the delta and theta bands associated with sleep and totally passive states, sixteen of the 'neutral' alpha, and twenty-eight of the faster beta. Then, in Krugman's own words, 'As the first commercial came on, the subject

looked up and an entirely new pattern or mix appeared.'
The ratio switched almost instantly to 21:18:15. Alpha had
remained much the same, but the proportion of slow and
fast waves had done a complete turnaround. A close study
of the EEG tracing showed that 'the characteristic mode of
response' to the TV screen had fully developed in a mere
thirty seconds.

Krugman repeated each commercial twice, and noticed
that the woman's response to all three was not only almost
identical in terms of brain-wave performance, but with
repetition her slow waves were increasing and her fast
ones decreasing. The ratio for her viewing of one of the
repeats was 28:15:12, a tremendous predominance of very
slow waves. 'It appears', Krugman concluded, 'that this
subject's mode of response to television is very different
from her response to print. That is, the basic electrical
response of the brain is more to the media than to content
differences within the TV commercials.' The response to
print was essentially active, while the response to television
was passive.

Herbert Krugman concluded his report with some reflec-
tions of the kind not often heard from members of the TV
industry, at least not in public. 'Television as experience',
he said, 'is deficient in that reality is presented minus the
feelings. [It] does not appear to be communication as we
have known it. Our subject was working to learn something
from a print ad, but was passive about television. [She] was
no more trying to learn something from television than she
would be trying to learn something from a park landscape
while resting on a park bench.' He went so far as to add
that TV was 'a communication medium that may effort-
lessly transmit into storage huge quantities of information
not thought about at the time of exposure, but much of it
capable of later activation.'[6] The Shoppers' Trance effect
mentioned above suggests that he was right.

The alpha state is the one described here and in the
previous chapter as the state we enter when staring at
fires, whether we are making great scientific discoveries

or not, and when we stare at TV screens. Perhaps it should be known as the slow state, because the replacement of the fast waves by slow ones seems to be more important than the actual amount of the alpha in between them. This seems to be a state provided by nature to help us generate our own imagery by becoming deliberately passive, switching off all the senses and turning inwards, ignoring what is going on in the external world and clearing the mind for whatever might emerge from within. This is also the state we enter when absorbed in a routine chore that requires no intellectual effort, such as washing up or mowing the lawn. In such slow states, as is well known, 'inspiration' often makes its sudden and unexpected appearance.

Now, if a waking brain finds itself in the slow state while at the same time being bombarded with imagery, it cannot function normally. Evolution has not prepared it for any experience like this. So what does it do? This question was studied at length by Fred and Merrelyn Emery of the Australian National University at Canberra, who not only fully confirmed the research of Mulholland and Krugman but went further than anybody else in providing an explanation of why television affects people in the ways it does.

'Viewing', they reported, 'is at the conscious level of somnambulism.' They explained that when we look at something in our normal waking state we are in fact looking at it in two ways. The right side of the brain absorbs whatever images come in and whatever emotional associations these may have, but it is the left side that provides the logical analysis and integration necessary if we are to make any sense out of the images and put them to practical use. A special part of the left cortex called Area 39 has the job of integrating what comes in and initiating any action that may be appropriate. The right brain, on the other hand, just soaks up images like a sponge.

It now appears that the left brain can be lulled into a sense of security by a regularly repeated stimulus of any kind, especially a flickering light. It then becomes 'habituated' and stops processing the incoming stimulus because it does not seem important enough to put to any use. This means that information taken in while watching TV goes straight through customs and passport control, as it were, and most of it disappears from consciousness altogether.

A survey was once carried out in the San Francisco area to discover how much people remember of what they see on television. Two thousand people were telephoned shortly after an evening news programme and asked to list as many as they could of the news items they had just heard. The results were astonishing: more than half of those who claimed to have watched the whole programme could not remember even one.[7]

It is evidence of this kind that reinforces my conviction that watching TV is a futile activity, and I am glad to see Fred and Merrelyn Emery dealing with one of the most often repeated defences of television: its educational and mind-broadening content. The very act of looking at it, they explain, leads to 'unlearning for today's adults and non-learning for the children'. All it teaches is 'do your own thing, without shame'. Educational TV is a contradiction in terms.[8]

This does not mean that imagery from the screen goes in one eye and out the other. It goes in and stays in, piling up unsorted in some remote area beyond the reach of Area 39. Yet it does not necessarily stay there for ever. Erik Peper, an EEG expert at San Francisco State University who collaborated with Thomas Muholland, explains. 'The horror of television is that the information goes in but we don't react to it. It goes right into our memory pool, and perhaps we react to it later, but we don't know what we're reacting to. When you watch television you are training yourself not to react, and so later on you're doing things without knowing why you're doing them or where they came from.' He reckons that the only kind of training television achieves is that of making people into zombies and conditioning them not to react to what they see. This is exactly what the TV executive quoted by Charles Siepmann whom I mentioned in Chapter 3 said would happen.[9]

This brings us logically to the subject of post-hypnotic suggestion, in which people also do things without knowing why. A skilled hypnotist can put an idea in a hypnotised subject's head and order it to be carried out after the trance has ended. Stage hypnotists are fond of making their subjects do something silly such as undressing on stage or kissing the person next to them by short-term post-hypnotic suggestion.

Albert Moll was a distinguished Berlin doctor who carried out numerous experiments in what he called 'deferred suggestion' during the 1880s. He was especially intrigued by the elaborate justifications his subjects would produce to explain their actions:

> I tell a hypnotised subject that when he wakes he is to take a flower-pot from the window, wrap it in a cloth, put it on the sofa and bow to it three times. All [of] which he does. When he is asked for his reasons he answers, 'You know, when I woke and saw the flower-pot there I thought that as it was rather cold the flower-pot had better be warmed a little, or else the plant would die. So I wrapped it in the cloth and then I thought that as the sofa was near the fire I would put the flower-pot on it; and I bowed because I was pleased with myself for having such a bright idea.' He added that he did not consider the proceeding foolish.[10]

There were two ways in which people sought to explain actions of this kind. They would either invent reasons for what they saw as a perfectly logical thing to do, as in this case, or they would claim that they had been impelled in some way. Now nothing upsets people more than the merest suggestion that human free will may not be all we hold it to be, and even Moll was unwilling to tackle this question head-on. He contented himself with a quotation from Spinoza: *The illusion of free will is nothing but ignorance of the motives for our choice.* Moll also admitted something hypnotists rarely admit nowadays although they know it to be true: 'We can with certainty, by means of post-hypnotic suggestion, compel many actions which the subject in normal consciousness would refuse to perform.' Such actions, he added, could be considered 'compulsory'. He gives an example, which also illustrates long-term suggestion at work. He told his subject to come to his house on the sixteenth Tuesday counting from last Tuesday and to be rude to everybody there. The subject did as he was told.

Moll was puzzled by the fact that subjects seemed to be in a perfectly normal state of consciousness when they carried out long-term suggestions of this kind. (This one cannot have been wandering about in a trance for sixteen weeks!) He thought he might be 'ordering a new hypnosis at a fixed moment', an idea that does not appeal to modern hypnotists who reject authoritarian approaches. For what post-hypnotic suggestion (long- or short-term) amounts to is nothing less than the remote control of behaviour.

One of Moll's many ideas that were somewhat ahead of their time was that a kind of post-hypnotic suggestion often occurred naturally. As he put it: 'Some externally induced idea influences our actions, feelings, etc, without our being able by any means to remember how the idea was, so to speak, implanted in us.' He gave an imaginary example of how impressions from childhood could take effect later in life:

> Let us suppose that a child two or three years old is often in the society of A and B. A is kind and gentle, B hard and unkind, so that the child gradually learns to like A and dislike B. Let us suppose that the child sees neither for a long time; nevertheless when it does it will still like A and dislike B. The child, who is now several years older, will not know its own reasons; it will not remember the former conduct of A and B

. . . yet the effect of the old impressions remains, and shows itself in the child's behaviour to A and B.

This effect does not apply only to childhood:

> We are often influenced by unimportant expressions we have heard, though later we cannot trace back the effect to the cause. Our conduct with regard to persons, circumstances and things is very often the effect of early unconscious impressions.[11]

Freud carried this line of thought further by claiming that symptoms of adult diseases could be traced back to long-repressed experiences of childhood, usually involving rather weird sexual attitudes in both child and parent. The subsequent emphasis on childhood traumas that dominated psychiatry for a time, to the exclusion of almost everything else, distracted attention from the fact that any experience at all, trivial as well as traumatic, can have a profound effect on a child. This is a very difficult area to research for the simple reason that people cannot by definition remember repressed experience, though at least we know in some detail what a soggy piece of cake did for Marcel Proust:

> But when nothing subsists from an ancient past, after the death of beings and the destruction of images, only smell and taste endure, frailer yet livelier, more immaterial, more persistent, more faithful, like souls to recollect, to await, to hope on the ruins of all the rest, to bear without yielding on their almost impalpable droplets the immense edifice of memory.[12]

And so on, for twelve volumes.

While I was researching a story on the American Food for Peace programme in north-eastern Brazil, I learned from a nutritionist that absolute priority went to children under seven, because if they were not properly fed by then their bodies would never grow normally. I also learned that malnutrition was caused by too much of the wrong food, usually manioc flour in that region, as well as too little of the right kind. So it must be, surely, with mental development? Can a child raised on a diet of mental manioc, which satisfies hunger but provides almost no nutrition, be expected to grow normally?

Images planted in the mind at an early age can go off like time-bombs decades later, as Proust has shown us. When planted in immature minds they can take the form of what Moll called 'deferred suggestions' that make people do things they would not normally do, and leave no trace of their origins. This process of image-implanting can be done deliberately or it can happen by pure chance, and we can never be sure exactly what effect any given image is going to have, especially if they are implanted carelessly. A vivid illustration of this was given to me by Dr Stanley Rose, a distinguished medical hypnotist who is strongly opposed to stage performances of the art. A volunteer had been hypnotised on stage, the trance being induced by a swinging pendulum held in front of his face. After the show, as he was driving himself home, it began to rain. He switched on his windscreen wipers, went straight back into trance, and drove into a brick wall. He was very lucky not to have killed himself or somebody else. This kind of thing, Dr Rose told me, happens far too often for his liking. At the Birmingham mental hospital where he worked for many years he was constantly having to pick up the pieces after a stage hypnotist had been in town.

The differences between being hypnotised, by a stage performer or a doctor, and watching television are fairly obvious. The similarities are less so, yet just as real. The main difference is that a hypnotist normally makes specific direct suggestions whereas television does not, except of course in commercials. The main similarity only became evident in the late 1970s when researchers thought of examining the two halves of the brain separately while people were being hypnotised and found that hypnosis was what one of them called 'a right-hemisphere task'.

Dr Crisetta MacLeod-Morgan, the researcher in question, pointed out that during hypnosis typical left-brain functions such as sense of time, critical and analytical reasoning and perception of pain can be greatly reduced just as typical right-brain functions – dreaming, visualising and generally using the imagination – are much enhanced. She seems to have settled the issue by making EEG studies that gave support to her predictions.[13]

If we look at her work together with that of her com-patriots Fred and Merrelyn Emery, who described TV watching as a predominantly right-brain activity, we have a new way of looking at the problem. What it amounts to is that television watching induces a form of hypnotic trance in which any image at all can take on the quality of a suggestion, and can be expected to work its way into consciousness in its own time. It can then cause actions that may be entirely out of character. The fact that the sugges-tion is indirect (except in commercials) makes no difference. If anything, indirect suggestion tends to be more effective than the direct kind for the simple reason that there is less resistance to it. Moreover, it leaves no traces.

David Frost once asked a studio audience if any of them thought they had ever been brainwashed by television into believing what they did not really believe. Not surpris-ingly, no hands went up. 'How could they possibly know?' Milton Shulman asks. 'Television's influence is much too subtle to be detected by its victims.'[14]

The Emerys put it even more bluntly. 'Television as a simple, constant, repetitive and ambiguous visual stimulus gradually closes down the nervous system of man.'[15] No wonder the industry has got away with it for so long.

6

THE INVASION OF IDEAS

'AMAZING NEW TAPE SEDUCES WOMEN!' The advertisement that appeared under this headline in several American magazines in 1986 gave an idea of the shape of social life to come. It went into some detail:

> She thinks it's only music, but she's being erotically programmed subliminally to love you! Is push-button sex finally here??? YES!

The advertiser, an outfit called Mephisto Metamorphics Inc., claimed that the music cassettes on offer contained 'inaudible hidden commands' that 'penetrate her subconscious mind'. The predicted result: 'Soon, she wants you with an overpowering passion and a throbbing determination!' The explanation: like hypnosis, subliminal motivation was irresistible since it operated undetected by the conscious mind, and there was no known defence against it.

Reporter Bob Greene thought this all sounded too good to be true and so it was. When he tracked down the author of the ads, who refused to be named, he learned that the tapes had not actually been made yet. Even so, 'Mr Mephisto' seemed serious, pointing out that subliminal messages were already being included in the taped music heard in shopping malls. Messages like 'I am honest' were apparently lowering shoplifting statistics, and if the method worked on potential thieves it should also work to the advantage of potential seducers, he thought. He was even working on a tape for married women to play in order to get their husbands to speak to them. This was all most of them wanted, he claimed. Asked if subliminal seduction was ethical, he reckoned it was 'probably a step up from trying to seduce her with booze and drugs'.[1]

I am sure it was, if it worked, which I doubt. Subliminal messages are indeed used in shopping areas, though precise information on either content or effectiveness is hard to come by. However, there is quite a difference between reminding people not to do what they already know to be wrong and bringing about an instant change in normal behaviour. Subliminal communication does work, as we shall see, though not quite in the way Mr Mephisto seems to think.

The word subliminal (from the Latin *limen*, threshold) means below the threshold of conscious perception, whether of a sound or an image. Subliminal propaganda made headlines in 1957 when it was revealed that a cinema in New Jersey had been urging patrons to EAT POPCORN and DRINK COCA-COLA in messages flashed briefly on the screen during the main feature. After six weeks, popcorn sales were up by 57 per cent and Coca-Cola sales by 18 per cent. To some, it was a touch of Orwell's *Nineteen Eighty-Four*, although all that had happened was that some movie-goers had been persuaded to do a little more of what they would have done anyway.

Stories about subliminal messages soon became regular space fillers in newspapers. When I worked for *Time* magazine, we used to do what we called 'dancing mouse' stories now and then if absolutely nothing newsworthy was happening. We would go out and find somebody who had done something unusual, such as teaching a mouse to dance. Some of the subliminal stories were hardly more serious. There were allegations that pop musicians were indulging in a seditious practice called 'backward masking' – superimposing messages such as 'I love Satan' on their songs so that they would only be heard when the disc was played backwards. It was not clear if anybody ever did play the records backwards, and if so, how.

Scarcely had society recovered from the backward masking scare than it had to cope with the 'embed'. This was a simple message, usually just one word, either flashed during a commercial or written (embedded) on graphic material such as posters or record sleeves. Barbra Streisand's otherwise innocuous album 'A Star is Born' is supposed to have all kinds of suggestive symbols embedded in its cover design. A TV commercial for some stuff called Drano showed water gurgling down a plughole while the letters S, E and X were flashed briefly over what could be considered a fairly unsubtle symbol.

Then there was Super Paper, which hit the market in the early '80s. It looked like ordinary paper, but had two extraordinary features. One was the price, nearly a dollar a sheet, and the other was the subliminal words printed on them. According to the makers, these came in two styles, positive (YES, BUY, PAY) and negative (NO, DON'T COME). The latter was for party invitations you hoped would not be accepted. The *Wall Street Journal*, whose dancing mouse stories are in a class of their own, took a closer look at Super Paper and had it examined under infrared, ultraviolet and oblique light. 'If anything is there', said a forensic expert, 'we don't have the capacity to find it.' The reporter wondered if the embedded messages were so subliminal they didn't exist.[2]

The first known casualty of the subliminal war was an Indiana teenager who went along to see the horror film *The Exorcist* at his local cinema. The film was scary enough, but it also allegedly contained subliminal flashes of a death mask. During the performance, the lad passed out cold, hitting his head on the seat in front and breaking his jaw. When he recovered he took legal action against the film's producers, his lawyer claiming that the death mask was a 'major issue' in the case.

Once a topic has been made into a dancing mouse story, it becomes hard to take it seriously. This is unfortunate in the case of subliminal communication, for there are those who have taken it seriously and put it to good use. In 1939, psychologist James Miller did an interesting experiment in which he asked people to sit in front of an opaque screen in a darkened room and guess which of five ESP symbols, of the kind used in telepathy tests, the experimenter was looking at. The screen, he told them, would serve as a kind of crystal ball to boost their clairvoyant powers. Results were amazing, but subjects were told that faint images of the symbols had actually been projected on the screen during the experiment. So they had not been using their ESP after all, but actually seeing the symbols subliminally.[3]

Twenty years later, two researchers from Indiana University repeated this experiment using a real television screen. They prepared a feature film so that an ESP symbol was flashed every fifteen minutes, and asked volunteers to watch the film on their TV receivers at home and record their guesses. They were told that symbols were to be flashed, but if they were just guessing they could only expect to get one in five right, or 20 per cent. In fact, of 103 guesses the overall hit rate was 34 per cent.

The researchers, sociologist Melvin De Fleur and lecturer Robert Petranoff, then carried out a real-life experiment in subliminal persuasion with the co-operation of an Indianapolis TV station. In fact they did two experiments at once. The first was to see whether they could persuade viewers to buy something, and the second was to get viewers of the evening feature film to watch the programme after it, a newscast hosted by Frank Edwards.

Slides with the words BUY (PRODUCT A) were superimposed on the film for two weeks, with a special commercial for the same product shown during the second week. This enabled the researchers to see what difference the subliminal message made to an ordinary TV commercial, and what effect it had on its own. Results showed a massive victory for commercial methods. Sales of Product A (a variety of bacon) rose by just 1 per cent in the first week and 282 per cent in the second.

In the third week, the slides subliminally ordered viewers of the feature film to WATCH FRANK EDWARDS. Results were marginally positive for the first two days, with an extra 0.2 per cent of sets in the area switched on. Poor old Frank's audience dropped from then on until by Friday it was 7 per cent down. For the remaining two weeks of the experiment, two other food products were advertised both subliminally and normally, and again sales shot up by as much as 500 per cent, as did those of a product advertised only normally.

The researchers concluded that there was '*absolutely no evidence whatever* that the subliminal messages broadcast in the present experiment had the slightest effect in persuading the mass audience.'[4] (Their italics.) However, their report raises the question that the subliminal messages may not have been perceived at all. Duration of flashes is not stated, nor is frequency. We are told only that the message slides were projected at 1 per cent of the normal level of the picture. (Presumably 'level' means light intensity.) This is very subliminal indeed, and reminds me of Super Paper. I am tempted to speculate that despite its apparent thoroughness, this was a non-experiment designed (no doubt unconsciously) to produce negative results. The possible biases of one of the researchers, described as a lecturer in the Department of Radio and Television, were not stated. We shall come across more examples of what I call non-experiments later, and it is important to distinguish between those in which there is no evidence of deliberate intent to deceive (as here) and those in which there is.

One subliminal researcher who is undoubtedly biased, though in a strongly positive direction, is New Orleans inventor Hal C. Becker, holder of several US patents in the field of what he calls auditory and visual stimulation. He set out to make money from this, and with the best of motives – to help people. After carrying out a number of experiments he became convinced that people can be made to absorb information 'at non-reportable levels', and he published his early research in support of this claim in respectable scientific journals. In 1980 he addressed a conference at Massachusetts Institute of Technology on 'applications of subliminal video and audio stimuli in thera-peutic, educational, industrial and commercial settings'. He preferred to describe what he was doing as 'human resource potentiation' rather than what some critics were calling 'subliminal seduction', though he admitted that his work could be seen as a way of 'changing unhealthy thoughts and ideas to healthy thoughts and ideas'.

Equipment made by his Behavioral Engineering Cor-poration of Metairie, Louisiana, was already being used in a variety of settings from offices and stores to medical and dental clinics. Although only one of his clients wished to be named, the press managed to track down others, including a New Orleans supermarket owner who reported a 75 per cent reduction in shoplifting after he had installed one of Becker's black boxes broadcasting continuous messages like I WILL NOT STEAL. IF I STEAL I WILL GO TO JAIL underneath the background music. At the same time, losses from cash registers dropped from an average $125 a week to less than $10. In Buffalo, New York, the staff at an estate agency were told every day by the same method that I LOVE MY JOB. I AM THE GREATEST SALESMAN, with the result, according to the boss, that revenue was more than 30 per cent up although advertising had been reduced. This appears to be clear evidence, supported by statistics, for subliminal behaviour control.

The reason most of Becker's clients were unwilling to go public was usually given as fear that the American Civil Liberties Union would picket, attack or sue them. The exception was the McDonagh Medical Center in Gladstone, Missouri, where a number of benefits had followed the installation of Becker's equipment. Restlessness ('steam-ups') in the waiting room went down by 60 per cent, while a problem that had bothered one of the clinics for some time – patients fainting while being given therapy involving somewhat painful injections of Vitamin C – had been reduced to zero. Harmony and co-operation among staff members had improved noticeably, though this could not be properly measured. One target area in which precise measurement had been possible was smoking in the staff lounge – down by 70 per cent according to a cigarette-butt count.

Most of Becker's work in public areas involved sound only, but he also made use of visual messages with a machine called the Mark II Video Subliminal Processor. This had been used on patients seeking help for obesity and alcoholism, and also on paranoid schizophrenics. He reckoned that if he could show his tapes on television he would eliminate weight problems in one generation. He also thought he could reduce car insurance payments by half with the help of messages targeted at bad drivers.

This was not all. 'When a specific behavioural attribute is appropriately and adequately addressed subliminally,' he said, 'it appears reasonable to expect a 10 to 50 per cent improvement.' He admitted that what he was doing amounted to invasion of privacy – so did a police siren in the middle of the night, he added. They both had 'a nuisance factor but good results'. ACLU officials were less generous. 'It's tantamount to brainwashing', said one, 'and ought to be prohibited by legislation.' *Time* magazine, in a generally favourable article on Becker, noted that 'many Americans would undoubtedly be outraged by any secret attempts to influence their behaviour for better or worse.'[5]

The man who did most to make subliminal communication acceptable was New York psychologist Lloyd H. Silverman, who made no secret of his attempts to influence his private patients for the better and published his findings in several leading professional journals. He developed a technique he called 'subliminal psychodynamic activation' based on 'symbiotic fantasies', which was actually much simpler than its description might suggest. All patients had to do was to sit in front of a screen at the beginning and end of their weekly counselling sessions while a single message was flashed at them for a few milliseconds, far too short a time for it to be received by the conscious mind. That was it.

When Silverman began his experiments in the early '70s, it was well known that some subliminal messages had far more effect than others. The greater the emotional content the better, especially if the message was related, however indirectly, to the patient's problem. According to the traditions of Freudian analysis, many of the world's troubles can be traced back to an individual's unconscious desire to reunite with the mother-figure, so Silverman came up with what has become one of the standard phrases used in this kind of therapy: MOMMY AND I ARE ONE.

In one of his best-known experiments, Silverman offered free treatment for obesity at his New York clinic to thirty overweight women aged twenty-two to fifty-nine. To test the effectiveness of his MOMMY AND I . . . message, he only gave it to half the women, the other half being shown the control message PEOPLE ARE WALKING, chosen on the assumption that as it had no emotional content it would not cause any unconscious activation at all.

After eight weeks of subliminal therapy together with conventional counselling, the MOMMY group had lost an average of 8lbs, while the control group had lost five. A month after the end of the course, Silverman weighed his patients again and noticed a relapse in the control group, which had begun to put on weight again. The experimental group, however, had lost another 3lbs on average. This was encouraging, but there was a completely unexpected development.

A year later, Silverman checked the women's weights again and confirmed that he had achieved statistically significant results. There was one woman, though, who had been part of the control group subliminally receiving the 'neutral' message to the effect that people were walking, who now turned up for her weighing appointment looking trim and healthy, having lost as much weight as any member of the experimental group. Silverman complimented her on her appearance and asked how she had done it.

'Oh,' the woman replied, 'since I came to see you last year I've been walking everywhere.'

The moral of this hitherto unpublished story, which Silverman told a colleague shortly before his death, is that the power of indirect suggestion should not be underestimated. It also shows that one can never be sure exactly what effect it will have on any individual. In this case one woman was affected whereas fourteen others presumably were not. If Silverman had urged her verbally to take more exercise in the first place she might have staggered round the block a few times just to please him (and awarded herself an extra chocolate or two for her effort). Yet the indirect suggestion of 'people walking' received subliminally was enough to alter her behaviour – and her shape. In this case the alteration was for the better, yet in the wrong hands it could have been for the worse.

In an early project Silverman himself actually did alter behaviour for the worse deliberately. He spent four years studying various different groups including homosexuals, schizophrenics, depressives and stammerers, and by using a variety of 'wish-related' stimulus symbols representing incest, aggression or anality he managed to increase the homosexual orientation of the first group (which the volunteers concerned presumably considered to be an alteration for the worse), the 'thought disorder' of the second and the depression and stammering of the remaining two respectively. Neutral stimuli, he found, did not have these effects while the 'symbiotic gratification fantasy' (such as the Mommy message) helped resolve unconscious conflicts.[6]

We have come a long way since the unsuccessful WATCH FRANK EDWARDS experiment. Pioneers such as Silverman and Becker have shown that when the right symbol reaches the right person, it gets the right result. Subliminal messages have been put to use, and it now seems likely that they have even helped save lives, thanks to a technique developed in Sweden in the 1950s and still practically unknown anywhere else outside the aviation business.

Ulf Kragh, the psychologist with the Swedish Institute of Military Psychology who developed it, called it the Defence Mechanism Test (DMT). To take it, candidates sit in front of a device called a tachistoscope in which images are projected very briefly on a screen for as little as five thousandths of a second, well below the minimum time required for an image to be fully perceived consciously. At first, viewers have no idea what the image is, yet as it is flashed a few more times some vague impressions of it begin to find their way into their conscious minds, and by the end of the hour the image has been flashed fifteen or twenty times and the viewer should be able to complete an accurate drawing of it and describe it verbally in detail. The examiner learns a good deal about people's personalities from the way they draw and describe their impressions, and can make predictions as to how they would behave under extreme stress. The images have been carefully designed to contain elements of threat and conflict, and the purpose of the DMT is to see whether people are affected by 'preconscious modification' to the extent that what they describe is not what they saw at all, the discrepancy being caused by 'defence mechanisms' that distort impressions or suppress them altogether in order to reduce anxiety. This can lead to a wrong course of action being taken, in the case of a pilot a fatal one.

The Swedish Air Force made the DMT a compulsory part of its pilot selection procedure in 1970. Since then, pilot deaths have gone down from 4.9 per 100,000 flying hours to 2.1, and there has been a similar drop in crashes in which pilots were killed, indicating that more pilots of aircraft that were about to crash were managing to eject themselves in time. Of the 760 pilots who took the DMT between 1967 and 1971, only 2 per cent of those in the low category – that is, those with the most serious defence mechanism problems – were still in service in 1978. The percentage of those in the highest category was 60.

Dr Thomas Neuman, the military psychologist in charge of the programme from the beginning, reported in a 1988 follow-up study that only one of the 138 pilots in the original high-category group had subsequently crashed, compared with 13 out of 91 in the lowest category.[7] High scorers in the DMT are, it seems, definitely safer in the air, and the test is now used in several countries (though not in Britain, where the RAF Tornado pilot loss rate is thought to be even higher than the 7 per 100,000 flying hours admitted by the Ministry of Defence). One of the few to have appreciated its potential value to anybody in a high-stress job, and not only to pilots, is psychologist Norman Dixon, a recognised authority on subliminal communication. He considers it to be 'one of the greatest benefits that experimental psychology has ever conferred upon suffering humanity'.[8]

What, some will be wondering by now, does all this have to do with television, which does not use subliminal techniques? It may have done so in the past, as in the 1970 Labour party political broadcast, but it certainly does not make regular use of it, and even if it did, so what? Labour failed to win the 1970 general election, after all.

I am not suggesting that television uses secret subliminal techniques designed to turn us all into zombies and make it easier for a tyrant to take control of the country. I am not fond of conspiracy theories, and with one or two exceptions to be mentioned later I have nothing against any individual in the industry. Indeed, almost all those I have met have struck me as honourable, well-intentioned and very competent professionals doing a job in which they believe. My argument is with the technology, not the people who use it, and my purpose is to show that the act of watching television – any television – has something in common with the process of subliminal communication. This must be understood before I move on to a discussion of some of the ways in which television achieves its effects. I cannot claim that it has any undesirable effects at all unless I give some idea of the means by which it does so.

To return to Dr Silverman and his overweight women; the work of the psychodynamic activation specialists has now shown convincingly that an implanted image can modify behaviour – for better or worse according to the image and the person receiving it – without the person having any conscious knowledge of it. This can also be done accidentally as in the case of the woman who walked her way back to slimness. That particular story had a happy ending, yet it raises a disturbing question: she started walking everywhere on her own initiative, or so she thought, and Dr Silverman never specifically suggested this course of action. Yet it was his idea and not hers. He had changed her mind.

Television is non-stop image implant. Much of the imagery cannot be consciously processed for two reasons: the viewer's brain is in a state in which logical and sequential thought is not possible, and there is simply too much of it for any brain, even one in a normal state, to keep up with. Yet all the imagery is absorbed, and the fact that it is not consciously processed means that it is absorbed in much the same way as subliminal imagery. It can therefore be expected to have the same effects. Commenting on research into subliminal communication, Norman Dixon has written: 'The most striking finding to date . . . is that subliminal effects appear negatively correlated with stimulus energy. The further below threshold, the weaker or briefer the stimulus, the stronger its effect.' This, he adds, may in turn be 'qualitatively quite different from that of a supraliminal stimulus.'[9]

The reason for this is presumably the same as the reason for the effectiveness of post-hypnotic suggestions: there is no resistance to them for the simple reason that we do not see them come in. They are suddenly there, like a burglar who has crept silently through the back door.

'Nothing is so powerful as an idea whose time has come,'

Victor Hugo is often quoted as having said, though it was in fact one of his translators who said it. What Hugo wrote, at the end of his *Histoire d'un Crime*, was, 'One can resist the invasion of armies; one cannot resist the invasion of ideas.' This needs some qualification. If we hear somebody shouting in the street that the end of the world is at hand, we can evaluate that idea briefly and reject it (although we will not forget having heard it). If the same idea is put in our minds camouflaged as a post-hypnotic suggestion or a subliminal flash, we cannot evaluate it, so we cannot reject it. We will only become aware of it when it turns up in our conscious minds as one of our own ideas. By then, of course, it is too late to do anything about it.

The Shoppers' Trance phenomenon mentioned in the previous chapter is an example of how the successful invasion of ideas can affect us. There may seem to be nothing indirect or subliminal about television commercials, yet many viewers use the commercial break for a quick trip to the kitchen or the lavatory while others will talk over the ads, apparently not paying any attention to them. As any hypnotist knows, such a state of half-attention is ideal for the insertion of suggestions, since resistance is at its lowest. It is not necessary to watch a TV commercial to get the message. A word in the ear from a distance while opening the fridge, or a brief glimpse of the product while settling down for Part Two is just as effective, probably more so. On the next trip to the supermarket, the cans of Gloppo or whatever will simply fall off the shelves and into the baskets without their programmed purchasers having any idea what they are doing.

Nobody would deny that television advertisements are made in order to persuade people to buy things. Presumably this is what they do, or companies would not spend such huge sums making them and having them screened. It is worth pointing out that TV commercials make as much use of indirect suggestion as the direct kind. Repeating the product name *ad nauseam* (direct suggestion) is not enough; there must also be the indirect suggestion that life will be

75

somehow transformed by buying the product. During my viewing years, the trendy thing was nostalgia – for good old bread like Granny used to make, or good old real beer like the stuff that helped our lads win World War I. I went on buying Czechoslovakian beer and Covent Garden bread, neither of which I have ever seen advertised anywhere.

If indirect suggestion sells products, is it not likely to influence thought and behaviour in other ways as well? The telly generation has been force-fed with images almost from the moment it first opened its eyes. Many of those born after 1950 have acquired most of their first knowledge of the outside world at second hand through the mediation of the magic box. Their upbringing seems quite normal to them since they have no experience of life without television with which to compare it. No previous generation has ever had any remotely comparable experience, and it would be surprising if this sudden change in early learning habits had no lasting effects. To claim otherwise is rather like throwing things out of high windows into crowded streets and claiming that there is no evidence they have ever hit anybody.

PART THREE

Why should one feel it to be intolerable unless
one had some kind of ancestral memory that
things had once been different?

George Orwell, *Nineteen Eighty-Four*

'Till at last the child's mind *is* these
suggestions, and the sum of the suggestions *is*
the child's mind. And not the child's mind
only. The adult's mind too – all his life long.
The mind that judges and desires and decides
– made up of these suggestions. But all these
suggestions are *our* suggestions!' The Director
almost shouted in his triumph.

Aldous Huxley, *Brave New World*

7
YOU GUYS

The Canadian philosopher and physician Sir William Osler once described work as 'the great equaliser in the world, the true philosopher's stone which transmutes all the base metal of humanity into gold!' What might he have said of television had he lived to see it? This too is a great equaliser – it enables millions of people of all ages to sit and look at the same thing at the same time. It is also the real philosopher's stone of the late twentieth century, although it does not transmute its base material into anything as valuable as gold. It transmutes everything into television.

News, politics, sport, entertainment, drama, music, cookery, gardening and the weather forecast all go through the same sausage machine and come out as identical sausages with only superficial variations in flavouring – artificial, of course. The taste may differ slightly yet the aftertaste is always the same, and as with the Chinese Restaurant Syndrome, the more we consume the hungrier we get.

There is one point about television that even the most skilled lobbyist cannot deny: everything seen on it comes out exactly the same size. To a viewer with a 22-inch screen, everything in the known universe is 22 inches wide: a war, a cookery demonstration, man landing on the moon, the Queen wishing us a happy Christmas, President Nixon resigning, Lee Harvey Oswald dropping dead, a beer commercial, a penguin waddling around the Falkland Islands, and of course the known universe itself. All human life may be there, but much of it has lost something in the process of being cut down to size, and not all of it is real. Seeing should not be believing where television is concerned.

Reporting the news, some might think, is one of its most important functions and one it performs on the whole very well. This is the impression it would like us to have, yet it is a false one. Apart from the fact that news, like everything else, is transmuted into entertainment complete with theme music and star newsreaders, television is quite capable of creating what it claims to be merely reporting. It is not the first medium to do this, of course. The classic example of the reporter as newsmaker was Evelyn Waugh's William Boot in *Scoop* who, unable to find the war he had been sent to cover, made one up from scratch. Forty years later the fictional Boot was outdone by the real-life Foot (Paul, editor of a newspaper called the *Socialist Worker*) who by amazing coincidence was reported to have been on the spot with his photographer when members of a hitherto uneventful Manchester to London march mounted a savage attack on their police escorts, injuring forty-one of them, three seriously.[1]

The television camera can lie with rather more panache. A reporter for CBS television was once sent to cover a New Jersey prison riot, but when he got there he found that what had been only a minor disturbance was all over. Undeterred, he managed to infiltrate the prison, set his cameras up and make it clear to the prisoners what was expected of them. Then, with some suggestive arm-waving like a conductor bringing in the orchestra with a crash, he filmed a rerun of the non-riot that was a great improvement on the original.[2]

A particularly outrageous case of news-creation came from Northern Ireland when some prisoners on hunger-strike were attracting international attention. A TV crew (not British) wandered around Belfast looking for some protest action and, failing to find any, persuaded a group of youngsters to start some. A brick was duly flung at a van that just happened to be passing through the camera's field of vision, scoring a direct hit on the windscreen. The van swerved off the road and crashed. Great television. Shame about the driver and his little boy who was sitting beside him – both killed outright.[3]

Dr Richard Clutterbuck of the University of Exeter has shown in a well-documented study of the links between political violence and the media that this kind of thing goes on all the time (though seldom with fatal results) even when incitement is not deliberate. There are two ways in which television can be held responsible for news-creation – directly, as in the examples mentioned above, and indirectly. The latter takes place far more often and the effects can be just as serious, as became alarmingly clear during Britain's 1981 urban riot season. This began in April with the Battle of Brixton, during which the petrol bomb made its début on English streets, and continued with the three-day orgy of violence in the Toxteth area of Liverpool. It can hardly be a coincidence, Clutterbuck notes, that over the next five days and nights there were 38 riots in 21 cities and 15 London boroughs, petrol bombs being used repeatedly all over the country.

A young Londoner gave this account of his involvement in the action:

I'm bored with everything around me. To try out for real what I see on the box is good thinking. I've been into all the fights, with the shop windows, the pigs, the lot. It's so bloody easy. That's what's so funny. It's as easy as watching it happen in Ireland . . . This is the London show.[4]

This particular boy cannot have been heavily into Pavlov, or he would have known that 'good thinking' is precisely what cannot be done after behaviour conditioning, provided in this case by television coverage in which all that was missing, according to Clutterbuck, was 'the seductive voice-over: *Are you bored? Do you want some excitement in your life? Why not join us? And help yourself to what you want.*'[5] So I will do what television does all the time and retake the interview after a spot of coaching. Let's try it again:

> I've become desensitised by regular repetition of excessive negative stimulus from my environment. Trying out what I see on the screen is just a form of ultra-paradoxical conditioned response. Know what I mean?

Yes, we do. The endless images of blood and destruction on the streets of Northern Ireland were largely responsible for the habituation and desensitisation process. It was indeed 'bloody easy' to reproduce the images of broken shop windows, burning cars and things thrown at policemen. Faced with a suitable sheet of glass, car or policeman, a properly conditioned televiewer of an age at which a certain amount of aggression is natural can hardly be expected to do anything else. Speaking at the enquiry into the Brixton riots held by Lord Scarman, the BBC radio and television veteran Sir Robin Day admitted that 'television may well have been, if not the cause, a contributing influence' to the then recent wave of lawlessness. Words he used to suggest what it might have done included 'inflamed', 'magnified', 'incited', and 'encouraged'.[6]

One of the most controversial items ever shown on the BBC was the interview on 5 July 1979 with a couple of heavily disguised Irishmen who claimed responsibility for the murder three months previously of Airey Neave, MP. They produced no evidence to support their claim and were allowed to give a plug for their then little-known group, apparently a rival to the Provisional Irish Republican Army. Ten days later, former Home Secretary Merlyn Rees took part in a studio discussion of the interview in which it was noted that members of the IRA would have seen the interview as publicity for a rival faction. 'Are they going to outdo each other?' Mr Rees wondered. It seems they were, for on 27 August the IRA murdered Earl Mountbatten, the Queen's uncle. The assassination of a Member of Parliament could only be outdone by the killing of a member of the

Royal Family, and we can only speculate as to whether this would have taken place if the BBC interview had not been screened.[7]

During the siege of the Iranian embassy in London in April 1980, and the dramatic rescue operation by members of the Special Air Service, relations between television and the news were a good deal more direct. To begin with, according to Clutterbuck the terrorists chose to mount their 'television spectacular', as he calls it, in London because they thought British media coverage to be the best in the world. They were probably right, and it lived up to its reputation. Part of the SAS operation involved climbing over the roof from front to back of the embassy and entering through a rear window. For this reason the police banned the use of TV cameras behind the building since it was thought probable that the terrorists would be glued to their TV set, and a single shot of a soldier abseiling down from the roof could blow the whole operation.

In the event, the whole operation came very close to being blown, with potentially fatal consequences. An Independent Television News cameraman managed to get into a building behind the embassy by persuading police that he was a resident just back from a trip. His 'luggage' was his camera equipment, and he filmed quite enough to reveal what the SAS unit was up to. Since he was using Electronic News Gathering (ENG) equipment, with which cameras can simultaneously film and project on the studio screen, his pictures could have been transmitted as they happened. Mercifully they were not until the siege was over a few minutes later, but with a less well-briefed, less ethically-minded or less wide-awake programme director on duty they could easily have been. It was an uncomfortably close thing. A BBC news editor described the coverage of the siege as 'one of the finest hours' (of television), borrowing a phrase from one of Churchill's wartime speeches with typical television hubris.[8]

We should not blame TV reporters for behaving as they do, says Peter Conrad, author of an erudite study

83

of television manners, 'because their methods are licensed by the politicians, diplomats and terrorists who are their subjects'. These groups 'believe in their own actions only if they see them on television, and have therefore taken to negotiating not with government agents or officials but with the cameramen'. The level of absurdity to which this state of affairs can lead in politics was shown at a Democratic party meeting in New York during the 1980 election campaign, where the media outnumbered the delegates by more than two to one and the democratic process was literally brought to a halt for the simple reason that delegates were unable to reach their colleagues and talk to them among the hordes of TV crews.[9] Likewise, when straight-talking Soviet President Mikhail Gorbachev was asked on his 1989 visit to Paris what he thought of the Bastille, he replied 'I can't see it'.

Television had taken over American politics long before 1980, of course, and even before the 1960 Kennedy-Nixon TV debate already mentioned. Media historian David Halberstam gives the exact date: 1956. The attack had begun in 1952, when 'for the first time television profoundly affected the choice of the candidates at both conventions.' This was the last election campaign during which the two parties could lay down the ground rules for coverage. 'By 1956', says Halberstam, 'that was past, no logistical decision at a national convention could be made without consulting the networks, the two were locked into a terrible symbiotic relationship that allegedly benefited both.'[10]

It certainly benefited television, the first among equals in this new relationship. It elevated newsreaders like Walter Cronkite of CBS to a position of national authority to which nobody had elected him. Thus Cronkite, announcing his retirement (or should it be abdication?) in 1980, promised to hang on until Ronald Reagan had been sworn in 'because I've inaugurated every president since Truman and I want to do one more'. These, says Conrad, are 'the words of a head of state who lends legitimacy to the elected officials by condescending to describe their activities'.[11] Cronkite eventually moved into higher spheres with the series *Walter Cronkite's Universe*, confirming that he and not God had created it.

The upper limit of television *chutzpah* was reached at one of Richard Nixon's pre-Watergate press conferences in 1974. At a delicate moment after Nixon had told what sounded to some like a thumping lie, Dan Rather of CBS got to his feet for what Halberstam describes as 'the ultimate confrontation between bull and bullfighter' to the accompaniment of loud cheering and booing from his excited colleagues.

'Are you running for something?' Nixon asked, surprised by all the commotion.

'No sir, Mr President – are you?' Rather replied. There were those who felt he had gone too far and should be disciplined, yet it was Nixon who lost his job five months later. Rather was anointed, I mean appointed, anchorman for the prestigious *CBS Reports* and given a 50 per cent pay rise.[12]

When Lyndon Johnson, after completing his presidency, was being interviewed in 1971 for his 'televised memoirs' he was asked what he thought had changed in politics in the thirty years since he had entered Congress. LBJ was in a good mood, as he should have been since he was earning a six-figure sum for his performance, yet his reply was both immediate and surprisingly vehement:

'You guys,' he shot back. 'All you guys in the media. All of politics has changed because of you.'[13]

Relations between politicians and the media are more orderly in Britain, yet here too politics has changed because of 'you guys'. Long before television finally battered its way through the doors of the House of Commons in 1989, the government had been lured into the TV studio in the form of the comedy series *Yes, Minister*, which many believed to be an accurate portrayal of those who made the government work. The appearance in one episode of guest star Margaret Thatcher emphasised the point: government had been hijacked by the entertainment industry.

Another instance of this was the weekly political chat show launched in 1979 and presented by Robin Day. Its title, *Question Time*, was a typical piece of television cheek, being borrowed from the real-life question time during which Members of Parliament have a go at the Prime Minister and members of the Cabinet. Day had stood for parliament himself in 1959, the year he joined the BBC, putting up a good fight in the Hereford contest and winning second place for the Liberal party. In 1981 he was given an honour relatively few MPs can expect when he was knighted, for his considerable services to radio and television. By then he had achieved a position in political life he would never have had even as leader of the Liberals. 'He talks to ministers with the affable menace of a polite equal,' wrote parliamentary journalist Edward Pearce in a tribute on the tenth anniversary of *Question Time*.[14] Yet even the ministers know who is in charge. Television is not interested in equality, but in exploiting every area of national life for its own purposes. The elected representatives of the people are just bit players. Sir Robin Day's obviously genuine commitment to what he has called 'the reasonable society' is some consolation to those like myself who feel that a potentially dangerous precedent has been set. The fact that Sir Robin has never abused his position of influence is no guarantee that others will not do so in the future.

Far from resenting television's intrusions on to their ground, politicians have welcomed it with open arms. Margaret Thatcher, Britain's first media-smart Prime Minister, began to work on her image soon after becoming leader of the Conservative party in 1975, hiring former television producer Gordon Reece to teach her the business. He did his job so well that he was made the party's communications director in 1978 and has been credited with playing the 'central role in deciding how Mrs Thatcher should be projected during the 1979 campaign'. He even admitted later that he had 'produced the product I set out to produce' and that she had been 'wrapped like a commodity'. For the 1983 general election campaign he had the help of newly appointed party Marketing Director Christopher Lawson, whose previous experience in the marketing of precooked meals is apparently what is needed nowadays in the conduct of democratic elections.[15]

Having perfected her image, Mrs Thatcher set about improving the soundtrack to go with it, hiring (and later knighting) playwright Ronald Millar who provided her with such headline-grabbing lines as 'This lady's not for turning' and 'Some say Maggie may'. By 1983, British elections had become media events rather than political ones, and it will take a challenger with even more determination than Mrs Thatcher to bring politics back into elections at the expense of image-selling.

It seemed quite natural for politicians to move into show business, whether presenting TV commercials for dog food (Clement Freud, Liberal) or cheese (Ken Livingstone, Labour) or hosting their own shows (Norman Tebbitt, Conservative, and Austin Mitchell, Labour). For Labour MP Brian Walden, the move from the House of Commons to the chair of a prime-time Sunday programme on commercial television was clearly a promotion.

As for the proceedings of the House, these were upgraded overnight from mere politics to show business. The *Daily Mail*, for example, greeted THE MAGGIE AND NEIL SHOW in its front-page headline on 22 November 1989. The full effect of this transformation may not be felt for some time, but there is a precedent indicating that television exposure has led to the loss of public respect for another national institution – the Royal Family, no less.

The Investiture of the Prince of Wales at Caernarvon Castle in 1969 was a major TV spectacular seen all over the world and one of the first royal pageants staged as much for the cameras as for those present. Milton Shulman found it 'a grand show', its ritual conveying 'that sense of remoteness and distance which is a basic ingredient of monarchical authority'. The remoteness was not to last, however. In the same year the entire Royal Family was brought into close-up in the BBC documentary simply entitled *Royal*

Family. Critics praised Richard Cawston's film as a model of good taste and tact. He and his crew had trailed round for a year filming the Queen, her family and her dogs, while Prince Philip told jokes, Prince Charles fried sausages and the Queen gave Prince Edward a lollipop. To be sure, she was also seen attending to affairs of state, but the overall impression was of a nice, normal happy family. The mass audience lapped it up, and it was left to Shulman to point out that a questionable precedent had been set. A few more documentaries like this, he said, would 'soon turn the Royal Family into inhabitants of the posh end of Coronation Street'.

Statistics supported his fear that familiarity had led to contempt. In 1969 a National Opinion Poll found that the monarchy was regarded as a necessity by 84 per cent of the British people, the figure being slightly lower (76 per cent) for the sixteen to thirty-four age group. When the NOP carried out an identical survey two years later the figures had dropped to 78 and 72 per cent. In the age bracket that included the country's first telly-weaned generation the drop was considerably sharper – no less than 14 per cent. The Royal Family had evidently suffered the same fate as the Church: increased exposure on the home screen had led to a loss of respect.[16]

This is the most insidious of the effects of the modern philosopher's stone. By working its way through all areas of national life, and converting them all into equal-sized images, it bestows a spurious equality on them. At the same time, it strips them of any 'sense of remoteness' and thus reduces their authority and viewers' respect for them. As a result, one illusion after another is destroyed as the Queen, the Prime Minister, the Archbishop of Canterbury and indeed everybody else are all found to be exactly the same size. Moreover, they are guests in the viewer's home, subject to being thrown out at the switch of a channel. The familiarity promoted by television leads ultimately to contempt for everything and everybody.

*

Having enticed members of the Royal Family, Church and Parliament into its cast of supporting characters, the Evil Eye turned its gaze on one of the few remaining areas of public life previously protected from it – the judicial system. In 1988, American viewers were treated to a new development in soap opera, which might have been called *Joel and Hedda*. The plot went like this: wealthy criminal lawyer Joel Steinberg lives with his girlfriend Hedda Nussbaum and her six-year-old daughter Lisa. One day, little Lisa is found battered to death in Joel's smart Greenwich Village pad. Suspicion falls on Hedda, but when arrested she is found to have been systematically battered herself for several years. She turns up in court to testify against the real killer – Joel. The trial begins . . .

Not a very original story line. What was different about *Joel and Hedda* was that it was true. The parts of Steinberg, Nussbaum and Judge Harold Rothwax were played by themselves. Shortly before the trial came to court, New York State had passed a law permitting cameras inside courtrooms, and the networks were not going to miss a story like this. It had everything – sex, violence, drugs, murder. It was going to be better than *Dallas*, and so it was. The networks even rescheduled their commercials, something they had never done before for a soap opera. It was another of television's finest hours.

The judge allowed only one camera inside his courtroom, but he had no jurisdiction over what went on right outside it. There, dozens of TV producers and cameramen installed themselves to cover the show, grabbing anybody who came out of the studio – sorry, courtroom – and asking for their comments on the latest action. 'Sometimes the comments were innocuous, sometimes not,' wrote a British observer of this legal circus. The judge came out with the understatement of the year when, after noting that while the camera reflected accurately what was going on in court, the peripatetic lawyers outside did not, he added: 'That seems to me to be very disadvantageous to the process.' It was highly advantageous to television, though, which was what really mattered.

As an example of how things are done in countries less besotted with television, in the same week that *Joel and Hedda* was shown in Britain, the trial opened in Stockholm of a man accused of murdering Prime Minister Olof Palme in 1986. By then his name and photograph had appeared in several foreign newspapers, but as far as the Swedes were concerned he was known only as 'the forty-two-year-old', names of the accused not being made public in Sweden until there is a conviction.

The methods by which television gets a foot in the door can be insidiously clever. It was first used in British courts for the best of reasons: to enable children in abuse cases to give evidence by closed-circuit TV without having to face the ordeal of appearing in the main courtroom. Then in 1988 a judge gave the BBC permission to get right inside a courtroom – not to film a case but to demonstrate how the closed-circuit technology worked in practice. That was a start. The following year the BBC went further by managing to film the Law Lords giving judgment. Soon afterwards, a special working party of barristers, headed by Jonathan Caplan, recommended that cameras should be allowed in court. They suggested this should be on 'an experimental basis', which some might liken to offering a child an ice-cream on a hot day on a 'money back if not satisfied' basis.

Caplan's group thought court TV was a splendid idea. Justice would not be at risk. Television would not turn the law into entertainment. It would not intrude or disrupt, nor would it affect witnesses or jurors, who would not be shown. It might affect judges and lawyers by making them behave better. It would be just as fair to defendants as public trials are. The group had nothing to say about the terrific free publicity barristers would get, though the prospect may have crossed their well-trained minds.

BBC legal correspondent Joshua Rozenberg asked around and discovered that not all barristers shared this gung-ho approach. Some felt that litigation would become more distressing for those involved than it is already, others felt that barristers would play to the gallery. (They should know.) Television, said Lord Hailsham, a former Lord Chancellor, was 'not a window through which you see what goes on,' but something that 'makes people behave differently – sometimes better, sometimes worse'. Even so, one of the first things his successor, Lord Mackay, did was to allow judges to appear on it. 'He's clearly just the man we television correspondents are looking for,' Rozenberg concluded.[17]

There is a small point not often mentioned in the discussions of live courtroom TV: what if the defendant is acquitted? Suppose that Joel Steinberg had not been convicted of manslaughter, as he was, but had been found not guilty and set free? What kind of normal existence could he have expected to enjoy? As a household name and face all over the country, there would have been nothing for him except to continue in the profession that had been thrust upon him – that of television personality.

There is another aspect of the relentless expansion of television that is rarely debated. My local council's planning department insists that when somebody wants to build something in a conservation area, there must be evidence that it will enhance the area. It is not enough merely to obey the letter of the planning laws. Why should the same criterion not be applied to television? What good will it do by filming trials? Or royal picnics? Or parliamentary debates?

None at all. It will simply offer its captive and passive audience something new to goggle at. As already explained, the term 'educational television' is a contradiction in terms – a hypnotised mind cannot be educated except by suggestion, whether direct or indirect, post-hypnotic or subliminal. Televising court cases will only add to what there is already too much of – entertainment – while catering to viewers' insatiable curiosity about other people's private lives. It cannot possibly improve the legal system in any way.

I have attended several court cases, as juror or witness. One of them lasted five days and included several hours of tedious questioning, in an incredible number of different languages, on some unexciting but essential details. It would have made terrible television. It would have needed editing down from five days to five minutes for *Trial of the Day*, which will of course include players' comments on the game:

> Yeah, Jimmy, the defence was *really* tight, but at the end of the day the prisoner's in the back of the van, okay . . .?

This will be more acceptable television, but will have little resemblance to what actually went on in court. Once again, television will have reorganised the real world to suit its own purposes, as was the case on 21 November 1989, when the first live debate from the House of Commons was screened.

To judge from the following day's press comments, it was the most far-reaching instance of reality-restructuring of all. The *Financial Times* went so far as to predict that 'the ability of the government to keep to its present course may be tested by the arrival of TV in the Commons', and that its fate 'will be decided in what is already a television election campaign'.

'The House of Commons that emerged on the screen at 2.30 p.m. was not one that seasoned observers would recognise,' wrote seasoned observer Simon Heffer in the *Daily Telegraph*. The *Guardian* recalled that 'the critics said the cameras would change the nature of the place and skew its proceedings', adding, 'and yesterday they were right.' In the same paper, columnist Andrew Rawnsley noted that even the Speaker 'seemed to be putting on an extra show for the occasion, as if some TV producer had told him "Bernie, darling, camp it up a bit for the cameras, will you?"' *The Times* quoted the previous Speaker as finding the occasion 'an exhibitionist's paradise'.

All credit, therefore, to anti-TV Member of Parliament Ian Gow (described in *The Times* as 'one of the warm-up acts' to the debate on the Queen's Speech) for giving away some trade secrets. A TV charm school had told him that 55 per cent of his television impact would be made by his image, 38 per cent by his voice and body language, and 'only 7 per cent by what you are actually saying'. He would also be advised if he needed a new hairstyle and where to get it, the bald MP added gleefully. *Financial Times* TV critic Chris Dunkley admitted finding it difficult 'not to admire the man for his timing and delivery rather than his politics' and wondered if he might be able to 'sell the great blank space on his head to a sponsor?'

All good fun for the millions watching 'The Maggie and Neil Show' with their afternoon tea. Once again, television had sold them something they already had – in this case, free access to the proceedings of government whether on radio, in the papers or from the public gallery. All that television had done was enable them to stare at their elected leaders at point blank range and develop an obsessive interest in their clothes, hairstyles and false teeth at the expense of the subject being debated. They could also answer them back, something for which TV viewers have a compulsive fondness, or zap them into oblivion by effortless remote control and switch to another channel. (STARS OF DEMOCRACY FAIL TO SHAKE SOOTY'S RATINGS, headlined the *Independent*.) After a few hours of such derision, denigration and surrogate bullying, is it surprising that respect for the 'stars of democracy' and, more important, what they are supposed to represent, began to diminish?

One way and another, you guys have a lot to answer for.

8

FLAT-EARTH TELEVISION

The camera can certainly deceive. It can be economical with the truth and it can tell outright lies. Seeing, as magicians know, is not always believing, and television has developed some mendacious magic of its own that fools most viewers most of the time, although its tricks, unlike those of magicians, are fairly well known.

It can lie with the best intentions in the cause of artistic truth. In 1961 a talented young film-maker named Peter Watkins turned up at Granada Television to show what an executive later described as 'an extraordinary example of documentary filming'. Set in Budapest, it showed the Soviet invasion of 1956 and the heroic resistance of the Hungarian people. The camerawork was rough, much of it being hand-held, and the lighting was far from perfect, yet it reminded the Granada man of some of the best World War II newsreels from places like Arnhem and Stalingrad. He was struck by the film's 'utter realism' and concluded that 'it could only have been shot on the spot'.

It had not been, however, and Watkins had never claimed otherwise. He had made the film a few blocks from Canterbury Cathedral, and all those Central European-looking freedom fighters were in fact English amateur actors. The executive, Milton Shulman, was astonished and rather ashamed to have been taken in so completely. He decided to show the film to a couple of colleagues, both film-makers of long experience. They too were totally convinced until Shulman gave the game away, whereupon there was a long silence.

'Oh,' said one of them. He went on to explain that it could not be shown in that case, because if it were nobody would believe the newsreels any longer. It was not shown.[1]

In 1967, however, Granada did show what purported to be a documentary to mark the fiftieth anniversary of the Bolshevik Revolution under the title of John Reed's book *Ten Days That Shook the World*. This, as Russian history students know, was written by a highly biased observer and contained numerous distortions and omissions as well as some valuable first-hand testimony. Granada bent reality even further by including scenes from Sergei Eisenstein's 1927 film *October* showing the storming of the Winter Palace in Petrograd which, as students also know, simply did not happen the way he showed it. Eisenstein was the supreme master in the use of powerful imagery, and there may have been symbolic truth in his scenes of jubilant hordes clambering over the railings and swarming up the marble staircase. The real invaders, however, swarmed downstairs to the wine cellar and drank themselves senseless.[2]

The real King Henry V could not have rushed into battle at Agincourt yelling 'Once more unto the breach, dear friends', because Shakespeare's script was not written until 180 years later. We do not criticise Shakespeare for falsifying history, and nor should we criticise Eisenstein. Genius can be forgiven almost anything. Yet we can criticise television for deliberately mixing fact and fiction, which it does all the time. Deception is inherent in the technology, as became evident a few months before TV cameras broke into the House of Commons, when I was amused to learn that Members from both sides were, as one report put it, 'rushing to enrol in a new charm school which for £300 a day will teach them how to look intelligent, thoughtful and well-groomed on television'.[3] In 1989, some of their constituents were having to make £300 last two or three weeks at least. Why, they may have wondered, the need to spend so much in order to learn how to be what an MP should be anyway? If they were unintelligent, thoughtless and scruffy, how did they get elected in the first place? Maybe they were anxious to correct the impression given by the introduction of live radio from the House, of a bunch of hooligans determined to prevent anybody from speaking?

One does not hear much about TV charm schools, of which there were at least twenty in Britain at the time. They were not to be found in the *Yellow Pages*, at least not by me, not even under 'Communications Consultants' or 'Media Training Courses'. Yet they exist. The Church of England has one of its own, as do the Army, the Institute of Directors and a good many other organisations. It sounds like a reasonable idea to prepare clergymen, soldiers, big bosses and anybody else who has to appear on television by teaching them some of the tricks of the interviewer's trade and showing them how to look and sound their best. Yet this is not all they do.

Michael Bland and Simone Mondesir, authors of a most useful guide to survival on the box, are disarmingly honest about some of the aspects of the industry in which one of them works. (The other is in public relations.) 'Undeniably', they write, 'television is *the* medium for transmitting personality.' However, 'it gives an immediate impression of someone, even if it's not necessarily the right impression.' Some successful people, they explain, simply do not convey what it is that has made them successful, just as professional TV performers can be disappointingly ordinary when one meets them off camera. 'Either way, television deprives you of your real personality and gives you a completely different one.' So, to be a success on the box one can be in only one of two categories:

1. Those whose image as it appears on the set is accidentally pleasing to the viewer.
2. Those who work at getting their image right.

If we are to believe these two experienced writers when they say that most people belong to the second category, it follows that most people we see on TV are unreal. If they have been through charm school and learned the tricks, the personality they project is not their real one but an illusion they want us to believe to be true. Bland and Mondesir cheerfully admit that their aim is to show people 'how to *exploit* television instead of being terrified and humiliated by it'. (Their emphasis.)[4]

The make-believe nature of the TV studio was brought home to me when I was plastered with make-up before being led on stage for the first time. I soon got used to it, just as I got used to the feeling that I was supposed to give a performance and entertain viewers rather than attempt any kind of serious discussion, as one still can on radio or at a lecture. I never bothered to go to charm school myself, though my publisher's publicity chief gave me an excellent crash course in on-camera behaviour on my way to my first interview.

'Don't look at the camera,' she said. 'Don't fidget, sit forward, and don't refer to "my book". Give the title. And have the last word.' Later, I worked out one or two formulas for getting out of tight corners including this guaranteed conversation-changer: 'Ah, you see, scientific research is about asking the right questions and you've just asked one of the wrong ones.' I also learned the trick of memorising a couple of phrases describing the virtues of my books and producing them during the interview regardless of what questions I was asked. Variations on that trick can be heard every day on radio and TV especially from politicians, along with such charm school favourites as, 'I can't answer that without explaining some of the background' or, 'Let me return to your earlier point for a moment'. Television performers have long ago crossed the line between wanting to look and sound their best and setting out to deceive. This may be acceptable up to a point in advertisements and authors' book plugs. I do not find it acceptable from those whose decisions affect our lives, although in a country obsessed with secrecy in government it should not surprise anybody that yet another technique for disguising the facts has been developed and that politicians are queuing up to learn it.

Another line that is all too easy for a television producer to cross is the one that separates critical examination of facts from deliberate distortion or suppression of facts. I will now give a case history from my own experience of what I call flat-earth television.

Psychical research has been one of my interests for many years, and it has been the subject of several of my books. It is also television's favourite dancing mouse story, which comes round about once a year usually on Hallowe'en. Sometimes the story is told straight, sometimes it is played for laughs, and sometimes it is made into a hatchet job. Since my account of the investigation by Maurice Grosse and myself of the Enfield poltergeist case of 1977-8, *This House is Haunted*, attracted an unusual amount of media attention, with more than a hundred interviews on radio and TV and in the press, I have been given an instructive course over the years in different ways of presenting the same material.

The case was unique in its class in that it was well witnessed and widely publicised right from the start, before I became involved. On the very first night, 31 August 1977, a police constable saw a chair moving unaided along the floor and later signed a statement describing the incident in detail. The case made the front page of the *Daily Mirror* on 10 September, reporter George Fallows stating that 'To the best of our ability, we have eliminated the possibility of trickery'. That night, the case was featured for two and a half hours on LBC radio, with the mother of the family concerned and her next door neighbour taking part. The following day on the BBC lunch-time news programme, reporter Rosalind Morris gave a straightforward account of events she had witnessed after spending a night in the house. She later compiled and narrated a well-researched forty-five-minute feature on the case.

So it went on. By the time *This House is Haunted* was published in 1980, the Enfield poltergeist was well known all over the world. Television had joined in early on, with accurate and objective coverage on the BBC *Nationwide* programme and in a half-hour feature made by BBC Scottish Television. The story even made the Thames Television evening news, on which presenter Rita Carter was seen asking Janet H., the girl around whom much of the action (but by no means all) had taken place, if she or her sister had ever played any tricks on the investigators.

'Oh yeah, once or twice,' she replied, 'just to see if Mr Grosse and Mr Playfair would catch us.' She added wistfully: 'And they always did.'

The press had already gone to some lengths to extract a confession from her. A neighbour has testified in a signed statement that a Sunday newspaper reporter offered her £1,000 'to say that what went on in that house was a pack of lies', while a representative of a daily tabloid promised to 'make it worth your while' if she could obtain a similar admission from Janet. She refused both offers indignantly.

One way and another, Maurice Grosse and I reckoned we had established our case. We were even paid a compliment of a kind in the 1982 film *Poltergeist*, produced by Steven Spielberg, which contained several incidents remarkably similar to those described in our book, though I have not yet been able to establish that this film was directly inspired by it, and have always thought that the film was never intended to be anything other than an amusing satire on American television.

By 1987 I had become accustomed to being approached two or three times a year by radio or television researchers working on some project related to parapsychology, and I had learned to be very careful before committing myself. Some of them had turned out very well, such as the film produced by Alan Radnor and directed with great flair by Rosie Bunting that included a good account of the Enfield case. Others had led to me having my brains picked clean by researchers who seemed to think I should be honoured to serve television in any way and not expect to get paid as well. Over the years I developed a sixth sense of my own as far as evaluating callers' real intentions was concerned.

The first call in 1987 came from a researcher for a company that was planning a feature on the so-called paranormal to be shown later that year on Channel 4, and to include the Enfield case. Would I take part? I asked who was in charge of production, and one of the names I was given was a Mr Karl Sabbagh. That rang a bell – two bells, in fact, and going through my press clipping files I found the ends of the bell ropes. Would this be the fellow who wrote an article in 1981 denouncing new methods of cancer treatment of the kind used at the Bristol centre inaugurated the year before by the Prince of Wales? More to the point, would it be the writer of a furious attack on the BBC *Horizon* programme in the *Listener* (29 September 1983) after its screening of Tony Edwards' film *The Case of ESP*, which Sabbagh had described as 'ninety minutes of gullibility in the guise of science'? The author of the article was described as 'a television producer and member of the Committee for the Scientific Investigation of Claims of the Paranormal', a notorious vigilante group specialising in slinging mud at anything not approved of by secular humanists. 'Unfortunately for rational thought', Sabbagh had lamented, 'we have not seen the last of this sort of programme.' He was right – he was going to make one himself. Well, well.

I called the researcher and told her I would rather not be involved. Meanwhile, Maurice Grosse had also been approached and persuaded that the film was to include a balanced and objective account of the Enfield case. He had agreed to make all his material available and to contact some of the many witnesses to the original events who were still around. He begged me to change my mind. 'If you don't do it, they'll find someone else who will get it all wrong,' he said. I knew he was right and finally gave in, thinking

I might be able to blunt the hatchet a little but knowing exactly what was coming.

It duly came, on Hallowe'en, of course. Our case was introduced by narrator Nicholas Humphrey as 'the most thoroughly studied poltergeist phenomenon on record', an important feature of which was 'the way evidence was recorded using objective scientific means'. That was nice, and so was the five-second shot of the book's cover which would have cost me several years' income if I had been paying for it. Viewers then saw Maurice and me walking out of the local railway station together, something we never did once during our investigations. This was followed by brief extracts from a long discussion filmed in Maurice's home. So far so good. The film then whizzed off into a story about some weird clergyman who had faked a miracle in order to encourage the faithful. Then came some fuzzy black and white shots of a girl of about Janet's age getting out of bed, flinging something and diving back under the sheets before yelling for her mother. This dramatic scene, viewers were told, had been made in Switzerland using a hidden camera.

'Poltergeist cases are traceable again and again to the tricks of adolescent children,' Humphrey intoned. 'At Enfield too you will remember that the focus of activity was a young girl.' Simple, really. Never mind about all that 'objective scientific evidence'. If there is no evidence, import some from Switzerland and prove that two and two make zero.

Viewers were then given a sample of the most controversial feature of the case, the male-sounding voice heard to come from Janet, who firmly denied producing it deliberately. Such voices are a common feature of so-called possession cases and have been reported for well over a century. We may have been the first to record one on tape.

'Maurice Grosse came to the conclusion that it was Janet who was making the man's voice,' said the narrator, 'but as always he accepted Janet's own remarkable interpretation that she was being used by a dead man.' In fact, Grosse had done nothing of the kind. As he explained in his interview, with the advice of a professor of phonetics, he had recorded the voice on a laryngograph and established beyond reasonable doubt that the voice was produced by the part of the larynx known as the false vocal folds. (Most people cannot speak in this way for more than a few seconds without getting a very sore throat). All of this was cut. Humphrey then took another swipe at our case by associating it with a notoriously fraudulent one involving the late Dr S. G. Soal (unmasked, incidentally, by our fellow members of the Society for Psychical Research) and summing up 'the whole story' of parapsychology as 'one of false dawns and fast eclipses'.

Maurice Grosse was having none of this. 'The devious bastards!' was his reaction when I called him. 'They turned the whole thing upside down.' He duly persuaded Channel 4's *Right to Reply* to look into the matter and the following week they did so, with Grosse and another disgruntled viewer in the studio and Karl Sabbagh beaming down the line from Dublin. Accused by Grosse and his fellow objector of bias, muddle, selective editing, negative credulity and deliberate ignoring of evidence, Sabbagh gave the game away in this revealing statement:

> The point about bias – let's look at this in a little more detail because people often get confused about this. If we were doing, for example, a programme on the shape of the earth, I don't think it would be a biased programme if on the whole looking at all the evidence it came down with a verdict that the earth was spherical. I don't think it would be a programme that spends half the time on arguments for flatness.[5]

Naturally. One thing they teach at charm school is how to dodge a question by answering another one with a statement that cannot be denied. The earth can be shown not to be flat in several ways, and no flat-earther has ever produced any hard evidence for flatness. Likewise, Sabbagh produced no evidence at all to support his claim that 'I think the Enfield poltergeist was a prime example of mental set, of self-deception and quite probably of fraud.'

There speaks the real flat-earther. It would have been a waste of time to listen to the testimony of those who had witnessed incidents they could not explain – the five members of the family, half a dozen neighbours (one of whom was sitting at home after agreeing to be interviewed while the film unit spent so much time creating 'local colour' with a specially hired milk van that they never bothered to go and see him), numerous visiting reporters and photographers, welfare workers, police officers, local tradesmen, not forgetting the committee set up by the Society for Psychical Research to examine our evidence – a total of more than thirty people other than Grosse and myself whose testimony would have been acceptable in any court of law. Not on flat-earth television, though, where the verdict is decided in advance.

'It makes scientists want to kick in the screen,' stormed Professor Stafford Beer after watching a so-called scientific programme in which no actual scientists had taken part. He objected to the way viewers were offered 'snippets of science at the producer's discretion' and concluded: 'The public does not get the real thing.' That was in 1971. Sixteen years later the public was still being denied it.[6]

'The more people get their basic information and values from the small screen, the greater will be the pressure on decision-makers for quick, volatile, palpable solutions to complex issues,'[7] wrote Milton Shulman, and this applies whether the issue is industrial strife, nuclear fusion, the history of the known universe or poltergeists. These are all complex and controversial issues, and quick solutions make better television than real discussions. In the case described above, a quick solution was clearly what some viewers wanted. Critic Christopher Tookey complimented

Humphrey on his 'timely and excellent debunking job on the kind of paranormal rubbish which is all the rage in the British gutter press', adding: 'The probability is, as he showed us, that the Enfield Poltergeist was a disturbed, attention-seeking adolescent.'[8] As if Grosse and I had never thought of that.

If some programmes of the flat-earth kind can be put down to a combination of prejudice and ignorance of the subject under discussion, this cannot be said of the most insidious of all forms of television truth-bending – the docudrama, or dramatised version of real historical events, sometimes involving people still living. An example of television's arrogation of the powers of the judicial system was the 1988 tele-trial of Kurt Waldheim, then still serving as democratically elected president of Austria. He had been accused of more involvement with Nazi crimes during World War II than he admitted, and a great deal more than was ever proved. The 'trial' was unusually thorough by television standards, lasting five hours and involving about eighty witnesses, and was made all the more realistic by the participation of a real and distinguished former Attorney-General, Lord Rawlinson. 'Before the hearing', he notes discreetly in his memoirs, 'some complained about the propriety of the process.'[9]

The scriptwriter for an earlier docudrama on the McCarthy purges has described the problems of condensing six or seven years of story into less than two hours. He could 'just barely hit the major highlights,' he said. One attorney's final speech to the jury had taken more than twelve hours. 'I had to do it in three minutes.'[10] No problem for an experienced TV writer. Forget the dull bits, and if the highlights are not quite high enough the editor can always jazz them up with some technical trickery. This is quite acceptable in a fictional presentation, but not in one that purports to tell a true story. Small wonder that the telly generation has difficulty knowing what is true and what is not, and has come to expect real life to be constant action, excitement and climax.

The news bulletins do much to reinforce this illusion, as they offer what Jerry Mander calls 'the skeleton of events' from which 'most of the information that a reasonable thinking person would consider necessary to any understanding' has been cut.[11] A TV news editor has admitted that his job is 'to cut out all the dead wood and dull moments', and writer Edward J. Epstein has given an example from his own experience of what this can do to a story. He went along to a protest meeting on an American university campus and witnessed a few speeches, and 'hours of milling about, in which the protest more or less dissipated for lack of interest'. Then there was about one minute of scuffles between five students and some patrolmen. No prizes for guessing what was selected for the two-minute item on the evening news. Questioning some TV editors, Epstein found that this technique of 'distilling action from preponderantly inactive scenes' was considered normal practice, not distortion. It was, one chief editor told him, 'what we are really paid for'.[12]

Of course. Real life is simply not good television. This was proved by an eccentric Californian who rented a small TV station in the San Francisco area, stuck a camera on a beach and left it there to broadcast hours and hours of waves breaking. Anybody able to receive the programme would have been within easy reach of the real Pacific Ocean. Perhaps the station owner was making a comment on the nature of reality? Actually being where the camera was would have been an experience entirely unlike that of watching what the camera was seeing. 'The experience of looking at oceans is beyond television's ability to deliver,' says Mander.[13] So is the experience of anything else. Television's only ability is to entertain, to cater for the generation it helped to create and condition it to 'skipping life's boring, troublesome, unlikeable bits, going fast-forward from one action-packed climax to the next', as Salman Rushdie puts it.[14]

This has even led to news being reported before it happened. In the 1989 elections for the European Parliament, voting ended on a Thursday night in Britain, but results were not to be announced until Sunday. This was not good enough for the BBC, who commissioned a vast exit poll and announced the results within minutes of the closing of the polling stations. This 'result', which was fairly but not completely accurate, was then discussed over the next three days as if it were the official one.

News has also been reported that probably never happened at all. In August 1989, tens of millions of Americans saw an exciting piece of film on ABC news in which a US government official was seen delivering a brief-case to a Soviet agent in Paris. The American, who was named, had not then been charged with any offence, and the man in the ABC film clip was in any case not him but an actor, as was the 'Soviet agent'. Not for ten seconds – an awfully long time in television – did ABC remember to mention that it was showing what might have happened.

'The fakery insulted viewers, ethics and journalism,' stormed the *New York Times* in an editorial. 'Television journalism is at risk of losing its credibility,' said former CBS news chief Fred Friendly, in a gesture of bolting the stable door after the horse had vanished over the horizon. NBC's Reuven Frank was more direct: 'It's marvellous for drama,' he said. 'For news, it's lies.'[15]

The credibility of CBS came under attack a month later with an allegation in a New York newspaper that it had shown faked film from Afghanistan. A similar claim was made against a British TV company by cameraman Nick Downie. The spirit of William Boot evidently lived on. At about the same time, two more instances of unacceptable behaviour on the part of both the BBC and London Weekend Television prompted a blistering editorial in the *Sunday Telegraph*, 8 October 1989, headed 'TV fakes the news'. 'In the past fortnight,' it began, 'television's news coverage has itself become news.' The London police had carried out a massive raid on suspected drug dealers only to find that the suspects had been inadvertently tipped off by a LWT reporter. (A 'member of the public' interviewed on the same day by LWT turned out to be an employee of the company.) The next day, Surrey police moved in to break up an illegal 'acid house' party only to find that BBC television had got there first. With an erudite reference to Heisenberg's Uncertainty Principle, whereby the act of measuring a subatomic particle can affect the way the thing behaves, the paper complained that 'television, by its very recording presence, alters events,' and warned people to be 'as robustly sceptical about the "news" they see on television as they have long been about the "news" they read in certain newspapers'.

By relying as heavily as it does on the various forms of illusion and deception that are normal and proper in fictional presentations, television forfeits the right to be regarded as anything other than entertainment in which it becomes impossible to distinguish between fact, fiction and fantasy.

How seriously should we take a medium in which history is rewritten and relieved of its 'dead wood'? One in which the news is operated on for the removal of dull bits or the transplanting of exciting material? One in which everybody from members of the government and judiciary to prime ministers and heads of state become actors and actresses professionally trained to exploit what in turn exploits them? One in which what is seen to happen may not have happened as seen, if at all? One in which the earth is not only claimed to be flat, but is actually shown to be?

9

THE LATEST IN BLOOD
AND GUTS

'After thirty years of television in Britain there is no
evidence that it makes ordinary kids into violent kids, or
that it bears responsibility for national crime rates.' At least,
not in the opinion of Mr John Whitney, director general of
the Independent Broadcasting Authority (IBA) who was
addressing a 1984 meeting of the National Association for
the Care and Resettlement of Offenders. A certain amount
of violence on the screen could even be a good thing, he
thought. For example, the bombing in 1984 of the Brighton
hotel in which the Prime Minister and most of the Cabinet
were staying 'produced a tide of moral indignation and
revulsion against the violence depicted'. Was that a good
cultural shock or a bad one?

If television really had any effect on anybody, Mr Whitney mused, 'we should now be living in a crime-free
society' because of all those programmes in which the police
are shown as tireless champions of law and order. He even
had a go at the police for continuing to point out that the rise
in British crime coincided with the rise in British television
viewing (true) and he went on to blame the whole mess
on politicians. 'Even home secretaries in both Labour and
Conservative governments have from time to time used
television as an alibi for the failure of successive admin-
istrations to deal with the problem of law and order in our
society.'

All their fault, you see. In any case, viewers were not
unduly bothered by violence on their home screens. Only

3 per cent of all complaints the previous year had even mentioned it, and that was down from 3.5 per cent the year before. (Three per cent of how many we were not told.) Moreover, 'in an imperfect society, containing violence in many forms, it would be unrealistic and untrue for television to ignore its violent aspects.' He ended with a skilful piece of misdirection and issue-confusing by referring to an IBA report in which it was revealed that viewers were capable of identifying 'a complex combination of factors in programmes they find violent'. Another major scientific breakthrough in the report was the discovery that 'different types of people interpret different types of violence in different ways'.

They do indeed. The headline next to the report of Mr Whitney's speech was: VIDEO NASTY LEFT BOY, 8, 'SHATTERED'. The boy had been on his way home from school when a friend invited him to come and see 'this smashing video Dad brought home'. The director of the Child Development Research Unit of the University of Nottingham described what happened next:

'This young boy watched a highly questionable and violent video film for only twenty minutes and was totally shattered and disabled by the experience. He simply could no longer control his own thoughts about it and suffered recurring nightmares.'[1] Here was an example of how one ordinary youngster was severely affected by some images seen on a television screen, although they would not have been shown by any TV network. It reminded readers that violent imagery can have profound effects and implied that the dividing line between standard TV violence and the 'video nasty' (of which more later) may not be so easy to find. The report also revealed that the Royal College of Psychiatry had undertaken a survey of members asking for case histories in which there might be links with TV or video sex and violence. It was clear that the case of the eight-year-old was not an isolated one.

Four years later the IBA issued a warning to Britain's commercial programme directors that there was still too much violence on television. At a meeting presided over by its chairman, Lord Thomson, it had been decided that the depiction of violence in some programmes continued to be 'unacceptable'.[2] They had not yet found that dividing line, it seemed, and I wondered why, if what Mr Whitney had been quoted above as saying was true, the IBA was still finding it necessary to discuss the subject of violence at all?

Mr Whitney's 1984 speech sparked off a lively series of letters in the *Daily Telegraph*, including one from me in which I questioned the claim that TV did not make normal children violent. 'This', I wrote, 'is precisely what it has been statistically shown to have done.' I mentioned the exact correlation, noticed more than ten years previously by Milton Shulman, between the increase in average TV-watching habits in the USA, Canada and Britain – the first three countries to pass the 90 per cent set ownership level – and the increase in crime committed by young people, adding that the correlation also existed in countries with less TV and less juvenile crime. Nobody had yet established that any factor other than television was responsible for this.[3]

Shulman himself joined in with a vigorous blast against the IBA. It came close to irresponsibility, he said, to try to justify existing TV violence levels by 'discrediting and distorting the evidence' that had led the three leading American networks to admit that television was a major contributor to violence. In Britain, Dr William Belson had reported in 1978 that 'high exposure to television violence increases the degree to which boys engage in serious violence' after questioning more than 1,500 adolescents. In the same year, Professor H. J. Eysenck and Dr David Nias had concluded after a review of all previous studies on the subject that television's contribution to violence was 'a powerful and omnipresent one'. A committee headed by Lord Annan had reached a similar conclusion. In the United States, the American Medical Association and the American Association of Advertising Agencies had done likewise. To allege that there was no consensus of opinion on the question, Shulman concluded, was simply not true.[4] Subsequent additions to the consensus have included those of the American Academy of Pediatrics (1984), the American Psychological Association (1985), and most notably the National Institute of Mental Health (1982) whose committee reported after a ten-year study that 'We have come to a unanimous conclusion that there is a causal relationship between television violence and real-life violence'.

I have left the discussion of TV and violence until now in order to give prominence to other aspects of the medium, such as the nature of the technology itself regardless of programme content, and to show that while violent behaviour is the most frequently discussed of television's negative effects, it is not the only one and is probably not the most destructive. All the same, it cannot be ignored.

The links between television and violence have been studied in four different ways: single case studies, field studies, experimental field studies and laboratory experiments. Of these, it is the single case studies that make the best headlines, like the one mentioned earlier. They can often seem very convincing, though Eysenck and Nias emphasise that from the scientific point of view they are the least satisfactory of the four types. They can serve as illustrations but not proof of anything. Even so, they do show what happens in the real world. For instance:

After watching a fictional film in which a man is beaten to death by his son, a seventeen-year-old boy went for his own father with a meat knife. 'It's just that when I watch television I sometimes imagine myself committing murders and thinking I can get away with it,' he said later, not having got away with it.

A schoolgirl of fifteen saw somebody plan a murder

on the American cops and robbers show *Starsky and Hutch* by cutting a car's brake cables. She tried to do away with her parents in a copycat replay of the episode, but unfortunately for her they came along on the crucial day to pick her up from school – in the same car.

Two viewers watched a break-in on a popular British serial and immediately went out and did one themselves. 'We saw how it was done on *Z-Cars*', one explained in court, 'and decided to have a go. It looked so easy.' However, real life has an annoying way of failing to stick to the script. The owner of the house came home and caught them red-handed.[5]

More choice single-case examples are given by veteran American TV reporter Daniel Schorr. They illustrate several different ways in which the paths of television and violence so often seem to cross:

A Maryland Vietnam war veteran, who once admitted 'I watch television too much,' saw an episode of a programme called *S.W.A.T.* in which a sniper opens fire at passers-by and is picked off in turn by a police marksman. He later went out and did likewise, and was also killed likewise.

Kidnapped newspaper editor Reg Murphy described later how the first thing his abductors did was turn on their TV set to see if they had made the evening news.

An Indianapolis man rushed out of a building holding a gun to the neck of a hostage. 'Get those goddamn cameras on,' he shouted to the eagerly waiting TV crews. 'I'm a goddamn national hero.'

Finally, we should spare a thought for the woman

announcer on a Florida TV station who came on air and announced this:

> In keeping with Channel 40's policy of bringing you the latest in blood and guts in living colour, you're going to see another first – an attempt at suicide.

Whereupon she produced a gun and made a successful one.

Single-case stories are of more interest when they form groups or part of a series. For example, following the attempted assassinations of presidents Ford and Reagan there were similar attempts or at least serious threats shortly afterwards. Said the psychiatrist who examined the second of Ford's would-be killers: 'People do get influenced by what they see on television.'[6]

Next we come to studies in which researchers go out into the field and observe what is assumed to be natural behaviour, much as they would study wild birds or animals. There were at least eight large-scale field studies published between 1958 and 1972, the first of which is of special interest since it was carried out when television was a new arrival in the British home. Dr Hilde Himmelweit and two colleagues from the London School of Economics began their work in 1954 and carried out several separate studies involving a total of more than 4,000 children. One, in Norwich, was designed to compare before-and-after differences in an area where TV had only recently become available. Such differences turned out to be minimal, and on completing their work the team was unable to produce any clear evidence for harmful effects of any kind.

This was just what the industry wanted to hear, and the Himmelweit report became virtually engraved in stone and regarded as the last word that need be said on the subject. Carefully edited versions of it are still being cited today by the pro-TV lobby, which overlooks the fact that British TV in the '50s bore little resemblance to the American product at that time, and still less to either British or

American programmes of even one decade later, let alone three. Moreover, some of Himmelweit's youngsters had been watching for only a matter of months. Her report could not comment on long-term effects for the simple reason that there were no long-term viewers.

Overlooked also are such comments by Himmelweit on programmes of the more violent kind as – 'We find little evidence that these programmes are desirable as a means of discharging tension (they often increase it) but do find evidence that they may retard children's awareness of the serious consequences of violence in real life and may teach a greater acceptance of aggression as the normal, manly solution of conflict.'[7]

Subsequent field studies have shown a clearly emerging pattern of behaviour modification as a result of viewing, especially viewing of violence. This is also true of experimental field studies, in which researchers interfere in some way with the natural behaviour of their subjects. This has usually involved making groups of people watch certain kinds of programme and comparing their effects, but such manipulation has often proved self-defeating. A normal group of lively youngsters, for instance, might well start to behave violently out of sheer boredom at having to watch several weeks of bland television.

Finally there is the laboratory experiment, considered by Eysenck and Nias to be the method of choice, because although it is artificial it does enable researchers to make precise measurements and generally keep things under control. Such experiments are inevitably restricted to short-term effects, yet they have produced the clearest evidence to date that ordinary children can be made into violent ones. In a typical experiment, a group of children is shown a film with an element of violence in it while another group is shown an innocuous one. Both groups are then given a specific task or just allowed to go out and play, and their behaviour is carefully monitored. There seems no reasonable doubt that violent visual stimuli have an immediate influence.

With adult subjects, experimenters have found some ingenious ways round ethical objections to provoking real violence by the use of various kinds of 'aggression machine'. In an early experiment, subjects were asked to help test the effects of punishment on learning ability, by giving somebody an electric shock whenever a mistake was made. They were not told that they, not the 'torture victim', were the real subjects in the experiment, nor that the victim was an accomplice of the researcher and was not really being shocked. The torturers thought they were doing the real thing, and the strength of the 'shocks' they were giving could be measured precisely. At a certain stage there would be a break during which the torturers were divided into two groups and given some light relief in the form of a film – a violent one for one group and a dull one for the other. In the first experiment of this kind, the violent bit of film chosen was the knife scene from *Rebel Without a Cause*, and when the fake 'learning' experiment was resumed it was found that the group who had watched James Dean doing his lethal thing gave stronger shocks of longer duration than before, whereas spectators of the dull film gave weaker ones of shorter duration. It was the first experiment of its kind to provide clear evidence for the disinhibition theory, and reviewing six such studies using various kinds of artificial aggression, Eysenck and Nias find them 'consistent in providing evidence that film violence increases our willingness to hurt or insult another person'.[8]

The value of experiments of this kind is that they provide the beginnings of an answer to the question of exactly how imagery can provoke violence. With young children the key factor is imitation, which is not surprising since young children imitate anything they can and much of early learning is based on imitation. If they see a film of an adult bashing a clown to a pulp and then find a similar-looking model clown in their playroom (put there by the researcher, of course) they will know exactly what to do with it, and will do it. In the case of older people the key factor is disinhibition, meaning that they will be more likely to consider violent behaviour as an option if they are given an opportunity for it while in a state of frustration.

It is interesting to see how the TV lobby simply ignores evidence while pretending to have discussed it. The classic experiment of the kind mentioned above, carried out by Dr Albert Bandura and colleagues, is dealt with in the IBA report recommended by Mr Whitney with this single bland sentence: 'Early observational learning studies indicated that boys imitated male actors rather than female actors, while the opposite was true of girls.' Does this mean that boys and girls really are different? No mention, of course, of anything else these 'early observational learning studies' indicated. Note the standard defence ploy here: faced with awkward evidence, avoid the issue entirely and state something blindingly obvious that has no chance of being denied. [9]

Disinhibition and imitation are not sufficient by themselves to turn an ordinary child into a violent one. The third requirement is desensitisation. This is probably the most important symptom in the television violence syndrome, and luckily it has been thoroughly studied and is well understood. It is often used for constructive purposes such as helping people to get over phobias or other emotional upsets. Eysenck gives an example of how it would be used in the case of a woman who was so terrified of spiders that she could not lead a normal life: first, she would be taught to relax properly so that she could become familiar with the contrasting feelings of tension/anxiety and relaxation/calm. Then the 'counter-conditioning' begins as the woman is taught to associate the idea of a spider with the feeling of being relaxed. A 'hierarchy of fears' is then used, starting with the least frightening spider image – that of a tiny spider seen a long way off through a closed window – and building up to the most frightening, a huge hairy monster invading the woman's bed. The woman is asked to visualise the least frightening image until she can do so without losing her relaxed and anxiety-free state. The therapist then moves up to the next image in the hierarchy, and so on step by step all the way to the top, perhaps even introducing real spiders instead of imaginary ones. The whole process may take several weeks, but it usually works. In this case the woman is desensitised spider-wise and no longer fears the things.[10]

The same process could of course be used in reverse, to make somebody afraid of spiders or to desensitise people to something to which they ought to be sensitive, such as love or peace. In a remarkably prophetic article published in 1961 and entitled 'Television and the problem of violence', Eysenck showed how it could be used to destroy something most of us would regard as a good thing – conscience. He began by asking what it was that stopped most people indulging in antisocial behaviour. Fear of punishment was not the answer; the chances of getting away with most crimes were reasonably good. Was it no more than a matter of 'conscience'? If so, what exactly did we mean by conscience? Was it a set of learned guiding principles as practised by religious people (and by the better type of secular humanist, I might add)? Or was it no more than an example of Pavlovian 'conditioned response'? If children are punished for being naughty, they become negatively conditioned as they associate wrongdoing with some kind of unpleasant experience in contrast to the rewards they get for being good. Whatever it was, conscience could be measured up to a point by means of the lie detector, which reveals the existence of our 'internal policeman' supervising our behaviour and reminding us when we are breaking the law, or even thinking of breaking it.

Now, said Eysenck, how would we go about destroying somebody's conscience if we wanted to? His answer: 'In precisely the same way as we would set about getting rid of his phobias and anxieties: by a process of deconditioning.' Viewing television in the home offered ideal surroundings for the process. Scenes of second-hand violence are shown while viewers are comfortable and relaxed, which they would not be if they were watching a real murder, rape or assault. The hierarchy of violent stimuli could be gone through again and again until none of it produced any anxiety response at all. An experience that would be extremely unpleasant in real life is presented in the comfort of the home in 'an attenuated symbolic form' and associated with food, drink and family togetherness. Thus violence becomes a normal feature of the home, like the wallpaper, the cat or Mother's cooking.[11]

Some seventeen years after describing this imaginary conscience-destroying experiment, Eysenck wrote: 'It would need a very powerful argument indeed to persuade anyone familiar with the extensive literature on desensitisation to take seriously the proposition that viewing large numbers of scenes of explicit sex and violence on film or TV would leave the viewer completely unaffected.' Those who claimed that such material had no effects simply ignored both the evidence and the desensitisation theory as if they did not exist.[12] How right he was can be seen by the single brief reference to his 1978 book in the IBA report mentioned earlier, which ignores the entire contents and merely cites an earlier work of Eysenck's on personality measurement![13]

Repetition is an important feature of the desensitisation process. Just as fear of spiders does not go away after a single hour on the couch, conscience is not suppressed with a couple of crimes on the screen. Pavlov had to ring his bells at feeding-time fairly often before his dogs became conditioned to salivate at the sound of it even when no food was given to them. What could be more repetitive than television, whether in content or the conditions in which it is watched? I have tried to avoid statistics as much as possible in this book. There is only one television statistic that really matters: there is far too much of the damned thing. However, one or two facts and figures are needed here. In 1985 the National Coalition on Television Violence, an American watchdog body, announced that average American sixteen-year-olds could be expected to have seen a staggering total of 250,000 acts of violence in their homes – on the TV screen, of course. Now, society has become more violent since the 1950s, but not that much more, although the TV lobby continues to insist that the screen is only reflecting society.

Milton Shulman demolished that argument back in 1973 by pointing out that even then the average American viewer was watching a greatly exaggerated 'mirror of society' on television: government statistics showed that the probability of anyone meeting real-life criminal violence during a whole year was about 1 in 400. The chance of facing it on any given day was 1 in 146,000. Yet on television at that time there were at least twenty-six criminally violent acts every day. Thus the 'mirror of society' was enlarging its violent side by a factor of somewhere near 4 million. Shulman wondered how 'a distortion of such gargantuan dimensions can be defended on the grounds that it is only "mirroring" what life is really like in the United States'.[14] One still wonders.

Another tired old excuse due to be given a rest is the 'Oh, but society was violent long before television' one. This is true, but it distracts attention from the question the TV lobby is not very good at handling: why has violence, especially among young people, increased so enormously since TV was introduced into their lives, even though most, if not all, of the previously known causes of criminal behaviour no longer apply to the extent they once did? Moreover, why is the quality of today's violence so different?

As already mentioned, it is interesting that violent crime by young people began to rise very sharply in the first three countries to reach the 90 per cent set-ownership level (USA, 1961; Canada, 1963; Britain, 1964) at precisely the time when each country's first generation reared with TV in the house was old enough to commit it. Shulman noted that these three countries had very different histories and traditions. 'What else had they in common besides similar systems of entertainment-oriented, violence-saturated television?' he asked. 'I await a convincing alternative explanation.'[15] One still waits.

Also awaited is an explanation for the fact that in Britain certain types of violent crime increased at a faster rate than they did in the United States, though admittedly from a lower baseline. At the same time similar types of crime went down in some European countries that had not reached the 90 per cent level, such as West Germany and the Netherlands. There is a nice little research project waiting to be done here. My prediction is that if the curves for TV home ownership for all countries are plotted together with crime increase ratios for all categories and all age groups, some interesting correlations will emerge. I also predict that the IBA will greet the results with the revelation that people are different.

No statistics can give any idea of the quality of telly-generation violence. I began to keep a file of news stories of unusually disgusting incidents in 1983, but gave it up after a few months because I found it too depressing. It included the following:

A young mother was out shopping near her home in Peckham, south London, pushing her fifteen-month-old baby in his pram when two men snatched her bag, after which one of them calmly stubbed out his cigarette on the baby's cheek.

A week later, another young mother was wheeling her five-month-old daughter around a Luton shopping centre when she was surrounded by a gang of youths demanding her money. The appearance of police in the distance aborted the mugging, but one of the gang found time to pick up the little girl, take out a pen and shove it into her eye.

Three men broke into a London newsagent's flat above his shop. So many awful things happened during a ninety-minute ordeal that his wife was unable to say later which was the worst part. For the man, it was possibly having one of his toes sawn off with a kitchen knife and being invited to eat it.

By 1983 we were well into the age of the video nasty. These were readily available for rental at about £1 from the friendly corner store to any youngster tall enough to reach over the counter. Delegates at a teachers' conference in April 1984 described some of the things their pupils were looking at after school: there was one video about ritualistic rape, another featuring the abuse and savage humiliation of a young girl, and a third that was a kind of instruction film in how to do maximum damage to human faces with knives. Mild stuff by video nasty standards, but sufficient to alarm teachers, paediatricians and psychiatrists as well as some of the children themselves.

It also scared the hell out of Members of Parliament, after a private showing of video nasties in the House of Commons. They passed the Video Recordings Bill (1984) in record time and set up a working party of educators and medical men and women to dig out the facts. It found plenty. For example, 45 per cent of all children in the seven to sixteen age group had seen at least one video considered to be obscene and subject to prosecution. More than 20 per cent had seen four or more. Some had been profoundly affected by them, psychiatrists reporting anxiety symptoms, depression, phobia, over-excitement, sleep disturbance, behaviour disorders, reality-distortion and precipitated or worsened psychosis. One intrepid paediatrician sat through some video nasties herself and suffered sleeping problems for two weeks. 'Right-minded people can have no concept of the content of these films,' she said.[16] Alas, they can now, thanks to a repulsive little book that somehow found its way into my public library in which several detailed synopses are given, all in the interest of the public's right to know, of course.[17]

Video nasties are worrying for several reasons. Most important, perhaps, is that unlike traditional fantasy-horror they do not show violence in exotic settings but in the typical urban or suburban environment in which their viewers live. But then they are not meant to be fantasies, they are meant to be real, and among other things they lead to understandable confusion in some viewers' minds as to what is real and what is not. One teacher described how one of her pupils had told her one day that Mummy had let her watch a nasty film the night before 'and now I know all about sex'. Asked what she knew, she explained: 'Sex is when a big man knocks you down on to the floor and gets on top of you and you scream and scream because it hurts.' When the teacher spoke to the child's mother, she was told, 'Well, she's got to find out about life some time, hasn't she?' The girl was four years old.[18]

Teachers questioned by the working party were unanimous in reporting a new and alarming quality of violent behaviour (and language) in their schools. One boy, disciplined for a series of savage attacks on other children, admitted to being a video nasty addict. He described one of them, or tried to, in writing: 'Four men rapped (*sic*) a lady and she got her back (*sic*) by killing very badly.' He continued, in philosophical mood: 'People can be affected by this and even go out and do these (*sic*) kind of things.' They can and he did, and was later suspended for yet another vicious assault. In a letter signed by six schoolteachers the point is made that 'violence and objectionable behaviour on the part of children is now regarded as being so perfectly normal that nothing very much need or can be done about it.'[19]

By 1987, an already bad situation had become worse, at least in Australia where a survey of 1,500 children in the ten to eleven age group from thirty-four schools found that a third of them admitted to having seen and enjoyed scenes of sadistic violence. Asked to describe particularly memorable scenes, they did, many admitting to having unwanted memories of them which they could not get out of their minds. They may have that problem for the rest of their lives. Commenting on this survey, a psychiatrist made the important point that the effect of violent entertainment is gradual, and most of its victims change their attitudes and behaviour without being aware of it, and hence without anybody else usually being aware of it either until it is too late.[20]

This is the whole point of desensitisation, whether for good or bad. Just as the woman afraid of spiders is guided gradually and carefully up the hierarchy, so is the television and video viewer guided steadily but also gradually towards an ever-increasing appetite for bigger and better thrills. Television executives may object, as I am sure they will, that any comparison between what is shown on television and privately-made video nasties is unfair, and so it may seem until we ask the question: who created the demand for the video nasty in the first place? Not the people who make them – they are supplying an obviously pre-existing market. Nobody would have bothered to make the things if there were no demand for them, and it is likely that the demand comes from those who have already been desensitised to the entire hierarchy of violence permitted on the BBC and ITV. Responsibility for the video nasty problem lies as much with the television companies for creating the demand as it does with the perverts and psychopaths who satisfy it. And what can we expect when the video nasty audience becomes desensitised to yet another high in the hierarchy and needs something even higher?

One of the most memorable films I ever saw was Michael Powell's *Peeping Tom* (1959), described in Leslie Halliwell's *Film Guide* as a 'thoroughly disagreeable suspenser'. Disagreeable it was, yet it was also a masterpiece. It featured a demented film cameraman who went around skewering women with a bayonet that popped out of his camera, and filming their last moments. The fact that one of his victims, Moira Shearer, had also starred in Powell's ballet classic *The Red Shoes* added to the impact of what may have been made as a rather black in-joke. Perhaps it will be shown one day to illustrate media exploitation of women? Anyway, this was a one-off, shown on general release, and I doubt if it led to any real-life mayhem in amateur photographic circles. I saw it only once and never saw any other film like it. Had I done so two or three times a week for several years, I dread to think of the effects I would have suffered. As it is, several scenes from *Peeping Tom* are still in my mind thirty years after I saw them, proof of the staying power of images.

Violence is part of life and art must obviously reflect it, and for most normal people there comes a point in the violence hierarchy where cut-off level is reached and they do not need any more. They may enjoy regular performances of *Hamlet* or *Macbeth*, each of which offer plenty of blood and guts. They may go regularly to the cinema for some action and excitement. They may look forward eagerly to the new Stephen King horror paperback. However, in the theatre, the cinema and the book violence is kept at a distance, at one remove from reality either in a special building or in the imagination. On television you have it for dinner and take it to bed with you. Moreover, the dose is repeated every day.

Small wonder, then, that the habitual viewer is guided from an early age all the way up the hierarchy of screen violence and then out into the world of real violence, where a vicious circle soon forms as crimes are committed, then covered by the camera which transmits its images to others who then go out and commit more mayhem. This is how stereotypes come into existence, and when a suitable opportunity arises for potentially violent youths, as at a football game, they know precisely what is expected of them as they act out their stereotype role without a thought. Eventually the vicious circle becomes a vicious spiral with better and better coverage of more (and more violent) violence. From time to time there is a climax that brings about a temporary halt in the spiral – for example, the thirty-nine dead at the Heysel stadium in Brussels in 1985, or the ninety-five crushed to death at Hillsborough in 1989. Yet the indirect effect of such climactic massacres is only to add to the general desensitisation to the point where such incidents come to be accepted as fairly normal.

Eysenck has produced a simple model of what he calls the 'aggression continuum' to illustrate his point that small effects can have far-reaching consequences. He assumes that 'predisposition to violence' among the general public can be shown on a scale from 0 for the completely non-violent to 100 for the completely violent, with most people somewhere in the middle and few at either extreme. He also assumes that somewhere on the scale there must be a band of people who are not yet violent but are potentially so. He now takes an imaginary group of a thousand people and shows them a very violent piece of film. This may add just one point to the Aggression Quotient (my term, not his, with apologies) of each. Not serious, one might think, yet it could mean that about seven of the thousand move into the violent group. If the film is violent enough to add two points to the AQ, then fifteen people would be affected. If five points were added, forty-four would enter the at-risk category. Eysenck points out that shifts of up to 5 per cent are well within the range of the findings of experimental psychology, 'even with single presentations'. A 1 per cent shift of the national AQ in Britain could increase the number of overtly violent people in the country by as many as 350,000. A 5 per cent swing would add 2.25 million to the total.[21]

This is of course an imaginary model which has been greatly simplified here merely to serve as an illustration of how violent behaviour can be increased. I need hardly add the obvious: the more violence there is in society, the more it will find its way on to the TV screen, thus more people will see and ultimately imitate it. It has been shown over and over again that violent behaviour can be provoked under laboratory conditions, and that such behaviour is imitative. This applies even to single presentations. Their effects may be temporary in the laboratory, but in real life with daily repetition and reinforcement for two or three hours, with anything up to twenty-five violent stimuli in a single hour (NBC's *Walking Tall*, according to the National Coalition on Television Violence), they can be permanent.

'It is clear to me that the causal relationship between televised violence and antisocial behaviour is sufficient to warrant appropriate and remedial action,' said US Surgeon General Jesse Sternfeld when he presented the report of his Scientific Advisory Committee in 1972. There was no such action. Indeed, there was plenty of action of a different kind before his committee even set to work, the TV lobby managing to blackball members who actually had experience of research in the field and had dared to publish findings unfavourable to the industry, and to infiltrate their own people. Victims of this purge included Albert Bandura, author of many books and papers on such directly relevant topics as behaviour modification, imitative learning and transmission of aggression. He was however called as a witness and took the opportunity to protest that the committee was being controlled 'by the very industries whose practices they are supposed to evaluate'.[22]

In 1984, a British headmaster looked out of his window during the morning break and saw something both new and puzzling. Half the children were gathered at one end of the playground, half at the other. A signal was given and the two groups charged at each other until the entire school was involved in a superfight. The headmaster dived in, grabbed a boy and asked him what on earth was going on. 'It's all right, sir,' he was told. 'We're playing police and miners.' This was during a prolonged strike in which police and pickets gave television a field day every day for nearly a year, and it was a neat example of how the 'mirror of society' is reflected back on society. I hope future games of this kind leave out the concrete block dropped at one stage from a bridge, with fatal results.[23]

Moving up to the other end of the spiral, we go back to 1981. In that year, former CBS correspondent Daniel Schorr began to have second thoughts about the industry he had served for thirty years and to express them in public. The attempt on President Reagan's life made him stop to think about 'the perverse effects of our violence-prone culture of entertainment'. The would-be assassin, John W. Hinckley Jr, was a pathetic misfit who seemed to have been influenced by everything from novels and films to 'fan frenzy' focused on a popular film actress. As he withdrew from normal life he retreated into what Schorr calls 'a waiting world of violent fantasy' in which he spent an increasing amount of time on his own with 'an exciting companion that made no demands on him' – his television set. Though it may have been a cinema film, *Taxi Driver*, that gave him the specific idea of trying to shoot the President, it was almost certainly television that took him through the necessary disinhibition and desensitisation processes so that when the time came for him to act out a lethal fantasy 'the screenplay was easily written'.

The television networks had set up a permanent 'presidential watch' ever since the 1961 Kennedy assassination. They had missed that one, though the close-up Ruby-Oswald shooting was some consolation and splendid television, and they were not going to miss another. Ronald Reagan was already a movie star, and with a pull of his trigger Hinckley was an instant TV star. Schorr describes how Hinckley later arrived at the federal courthouse to be charged, in a presidential-style motorcade, police sirens and all. 'No one could doubt his importance or challenge his identity.' If Descartes were alive today, Schorr adds, he might say 'I appear on television, therefore I am.'

The court hearing was 'great made-for-TV drama' in which not only Hinckley but White House aides, TV anchormen and the courageous President himself 'seemed to play assigned roles, as if caught up in some ineluctable screenplay'. Reagan won worldwide admiration for a 'flawless performance as the wisecracking, death-defying leader of the Free World', and yet ironically in doing so he helped to reinforce 'the pervasive sense of unreality engendered by a generation of television shoot-outs – the impression that being shot doesn't really hurt, that everything will turn out right in time for the final commercial'. It was yet another exercise in the sanitisation of violence and the blending of fantasy with real life. The media President was 'as much a product of the age of unreality' as the media freak who tried to kill him. The attack, planned as a media event, had been fed into the system to push the hierarchical spiral to new heights.

'In the media age,' Schorr concludes sadly, 'reality had been the first casualty.'[24]

10

OH, ANGIE!

On 27 February 1986 a London woman named Angie tried to kill herself after discovering that her husband was having yet another extramarital affair. She bought a large bottle of aspirin, put a handful into her mouth and washed the pills down with a gulp of her favourite medicine, neat gin. Angie and her publican husband 'Dirty' Den were, as most of Britain will remember, two of the characters from the BBC soap opera *EastEnders*. Her unsuccessful suicide attempt, or 'parasuicide', was watched by 14.4 million people – about 28 per cent of the population of the entire United Kingdom over four years of age. It was cut from the omnibus repeat version of the programme shown three days later and seen by a mere 9 million.

At Hackney Hospital in the real East End of London the total number of deliberate overdose cases admitted during the following week went up by 300 per cent. For Drs Simon Ellis and Susan Walsh in the accident and emergency department, this was 'the straw that broke the camel's back'. They were already short of beds and had to declare a 'yellow alert' resulting in the cancellation of routine admissions. In a letter to the *Lancet* they suggested that the BBC should contribute towards the extra cost it had caused their local health authority, and asked whether the programmers had considered 'the likely consequences of screening self-destructive behaviour that is likely to be copied?' They added: 'Next time, could they please arrange for Angie to take an overdose in the summer, when our bed state is not so acute?'[1]

Three doctors from Nottingham's University Hospital reported some equally suggestive findings. In the ten weeks before the screening of Angie's overdose they had been receiving between 14 and 30 similar cases a week, marginally less than the average for the same period in the previous six years (range 20 to 28). For the week after the screening the number shot up to 43. They felt that the increase could well be attributable to television. At about the same time as the near-fatal *EastEnders* incident, they noted, Channel 4 was showing its own soap opera *Brookside* in which there was an example of what might be seen as parasuicidal behaviour, albeit behind a closed door. They were concerned by the fact that the outcome of both episodes was a favourable one, giving the indirect suggestion that attempted suicide could be good for people by attracting sympathy and improving marital relations. They also showed professional interest in the BBC scriptwriters' ideas of normal hospital practice, noting that Angie had spent only twelve hours in hospital where 'presumably she underwent gastric lavage (not shown), and when she was allowed home later that day she looked only slightly the worse for wear'.[2]

More evidence came in, this time from Newcastle upon Tyne where overdose admissions in one hospital went up fivefold in the week beginning 2 March. Attendances for the whole city rose from 8 to 19 in the eight weeks before the programme to 35 in the week of the screening and a range of 16 to 26 for the following five weeks. Dr B. P. Fowler found Angie's rapid recovery 'exceptional', her self-discharge 'unusual' and her husband's change of attitude after the suicide attempt 'wholly unrealistic'.[3]

Was Angie driving the nation towards self-slaughter? Some thought so. A coroner publicly denounced the BBC for giving viewers the impression that parasuicide by overdose is quite safe if people think they will be found in time and saved. Even the *British Medical Journal* joined in the debate, quoting a statistician's estimate of the probability of the Nottingham and Hackney figures being due to chance alone at 1 in 10,000 and 1 in 100,000 respectively.[4]

Research sociologist Dr Stephen Platt of the University of Edinburgh decided to look into the matter more thoroughly. He collected data from sixty-three urban hospitals around the country and drew up a chart showing all cases of deliberate overdose admissions to about 40 per cent of Britain's larger hospitals for the eighteen days before Angie's parasuicide and the thirteen days after the omnibus repeat. To serve as a comparison, he also obtained the statistics for the previous year.

His findings were interesting. For Day 19 (the day after Angie's attempt) the number of cases around the country was up by 15 per cent on those for Day 18. They rose again by no less than 31 per cent on Day 22, the day after the omnibus showing in which the actual attempt had not been shown. Dr Platt wondered if this was a 'lagged' effect of the original episode. He also wondered why the largest increase was among men of forty-five or over and not in the group that might have been expected to identify with Angie, who was thought to be around forty, nor among supposedly more impressionable younger men or women. Another mystery was that increases were greatest in areas furthest from London; in London itself the overall rate actually went down by 7 per cent, although in Yorkshire and the north-east it rose by 36 per cent. Dr Platt felt obliged to conclude that the case against Angie was 'not proven'.[5]

Finally, the two doctors who had started all the fuss published a partial recantation in July 1987. With three colleagues and a research grant from the Independent Broadcasting Authority they took a closer look at their original statistics and concluded that Angie was unlikely to have provoked imitative behaviour, though they admitted that the cause of the increase in overdose cases in the first quarter of 1986 remained 'unclear'. Angie could not have been solely responsible, since the increase at two London hospitals had begun well before her overdose. It could, I suppose, be said that some viewers must have known she would be driven to suicide sooner or later the way Dirty Den was carrying on.[6]

Before the television lobby starts telling us that there is no evidence to suggest a link between screened suicide and the real thing, they might like to consider a couple of earlier cases in which considerably higher-risk groups were involved and in which the evidence is a good deal clearer.

In February 1985, ABC Television in the States broadcast a fictional film called *Surviving*, which showed how the successful suicide of an adolescent couple affected their parents. Before the screening, ABC put out a warning that parents should not let their children watch it unaccompanied, which suggests that the network was well aware that the film could have adverse effects on impressionable viewers, as indeed it did.

The film, the fourth in a series dealing with aspects of suicide, was shown on 10 February. Two days later a hospital in Waterbury, Connecticut, admitted a teenage boy and girl who had seen the show together and immediately planned to imitate it, fortunately without success. Over the next two weeks there were 12 more suicide attempt cases, and the final total for the month was 16, more than 8 times the average for the preceding twelve months.[7]

At about the same time, two child psychiatrists from Columbia University were digging out the figures for both successful and failed suicides for the two-week periods before and after the showing of each of the four films. They found that the mean number for attempts in the greater New York area was 14 for the pre-film fortnight and 21 in the two weeks after the film was shown. Moreover, there was 'a significant excess in completed suicides when compared with the number predicted'. They concluded that 'the results are consistent with the hypothesis that some teenage suicides are imitative.'[8]

When their report was published, the Connecticut doctors followed up their 16 February patients and asked them if they had seen the film. They all had.[9]

From Mannheim in West Germany came still clearer evidence that fictional TV suicide can lead to a real-life increase. There, doctors at the Central Institute for

Mental Health noted the effects of a six-part serial called *Death of a Student*, the climax of which was a boy's fatal leap in front of a train. The actual suicide was shown in each of the six episodes, thereby considerably reinforcing the original image. The result: 'A considerable increase in suicides committed in the same manner during the series and immediately after.' The largest increase in train-suicides was in 'population groups most closely resembling the fictional model in age and sex'.[10]

In fairness, it must be said that there have been several studies of TV fictional suicide programmes that have not been found to have any detectable effects. There are many possible reasons. One is that some programmes have offered a strong counter-suggestion, such as the eleven-episode 1972 series which dramatised the pioneering work of the Rev. Chad Varah's Samaritans suicide-prevention service. Only one episode actually ended in a death, and suicide rates did not go up although a good many more people got in touch with the Samaritans.[11]

Another very likely reason is that suicide rates vary widely among different age groups and in different countries. The student age is a notoriously high-risk one, and West German national rates are about twice those of Britain and the United States, so a TV film about a German student suicide can be expected to have more effect than one about a British woman of forty. Moreover, Angie's failed suicide attempt was shown only once, whereas the successful German one was shown six times. It amounted virtually to an advertisement for self-destruction.

Famous fictional suicides of the pre-television age include those of Romeo and Juliet, Goethe's Werther, Alfred de Vigny's Chatterton and Tolstoy's Anna Karenina. Two at least of these had considerable influence on their contemporaries. De Vigny was held responsible for doubling the French suicide rate in the 1830s, while Werther imitations became something of an epidemic. One sorrowful young man even left the book open at the relevant page in case anybody missed the connection. It would not be

surprising, therefore, if fictional suicide on television sometimes exercised a fatal influence on viewers. The fact that
it does not always do so should not detract attention from
the fact that sometimes it does.

We had not heard the last of Angie's off-screen influence following her rapid recovery from parasuicide. In
November 1986 she was again held responsible for shaping the nation's behaviour, though this time in a rather
more constructive way. Earlier that year, she and wayward
husband Den had apparently tried to get their marriage back
together and had been to see a marriage guidance counsel-
lor. Branches of the National Marriage Guidance Council
(NMGC) reported a sudden increase of up to 50 per cent
in the number of callers in need of their services.

According to an NMGC official, soap operas influence
people in a number of ways. They can prompt people to
examine their own relationships and bring problems into
the open, but they can also make such things as divorce
or having an affair seem more acceptable. Whether this is
a good or a bad influence must be a matter of opinion. The
official added that it was not that more people are unhappily
married today, but that they are less inclined to 'soldier on'
and more prone to go for the quick solution of divorce.[12]
This does not surprise me at all. The telly generation has
been conditioned to go for instant gratification without any
thought for the consequences.

If Angie prompted potential divorcees to try to save
their marriages, good for her. There can be little doubt
that broken homes have a far more destructive effect on
individuals and society than their breakers are willing to
admit, and it seems very likely that Angie helped bring
about repairs to a number of homes in danger of breaking
up. If she had a positive influence on this occasion, however,
it seems equally likely that she had a negative one earlier in
the year. I am left wondering just how many effects television might be having on people of which they are wholly
unaware.

When we turn to the effects of real suicide stories, the

evidence becomes a great deal better. This is largely due
to David P. Phillips, sociology professor at the University
of California at San Diego, who has been studying media
influences on self-destruction since 1974 and reports that
'the evidence strongly suggests that non-fictional suicide
stories elicit imitative suicide'. In that year he published
an article showing that the US suicide rate would go
up immediately after a case had been publicised in the
newspapers, but only if the story made the front page
and if the fact of suicide was specifically mentioned in
the headline. The increase was proportionally largest for
teenagers though other age groups were also affected, and
it was also largest in areas where the story had been most
widely publicised. To those who complained that the extra
suicides would have taken place anyway sooner or later,
Phillips pointed out that if this were the explanation there
should be a drop following the post-publicity peak, but no
such drop was to be found. The largest increase, incidentally, followed the death of Marilyn Monroe, which was
announced as a suicide although it was later suggested that
the correct verdict was murder.[13]

Later, Phillips did similar surveys using televised news
stories about suicide instead of printed ones, and came up
with similar results. Again, teenagers proved the most
susceptible, and the effect seemed to last for about ten
days. As the evidence piled up in study after study, the
television networks seemed to have become alarmed. In
1988, a study sponsored by the National Broadcasting
Company (NBC) came out with negative results. It
looked to me like a study that was meant from the start
to have negative results, because it made no distinction
between stories heavily publicised on more than one TV
channel and those merely mentioned once. Phillips had
already shown that the way in which a story is publicised,
whether in a newspaper or on television, is just as important as the story itself. Thus NBC managed to disprove a
claim that neither Phillips nor anybody else had made in
the first place. There is quite a lot of this kind of thing in

science, particularly where vested interests are involved.[14]

One of Phillips's most intriguing discoveries is that there seems to be a suicidal component in road accidents. Most drivers would agree that some people drive as if they were trying to kill themselves, and the statistics now indicate that they really do. Phillips went through five California newspapers from 1966 to 1973 and found twenty-three front-page stories about individual suicides. He then obtained the figures for fatal road accidents in the state and worked out how many deaths could have been predicted in any given week on the basis of figures for the same week in previous years.

For example, in November 1970 the Japanese novelist Yukio Mishima took his own life hy hara-kiri, attracting tremendous publicity. In the week following his death, there were 117 road fatalities in California, 18 per cent more than the expected number of 99. There were increases after 18 of the 23 front-page stories, one as high as 36 per cent. Again, Phillips found a correlation between the level of coverage and the casualty increase.[15]

This interesting survey emphasises the point that some suicides are more influential than others. I would guess that the deaths of an Egyptian general and a Chinese army leader did not affect Californians of any age group very much – the road death toll went down after each of their suicides. On the other hand, the dramatic self-burning of Czech student patriot Jan Palach in 1969 may well have struck a chord in those who were opposed to oppression in whatever political form. Palach's death was given wider newspaper coverage than any other in Phillips's list, and in the week after it road deaths in California went up by 30 per cent.[16]

Phillips uses the phrase 'natural advertisements' to describe widely publicised suicide stories. This raises the question that just about anything shown on television can be seen as an advertisement, however well disguised. If this is so, then non-commercial stations such as the BBC are in the selling business just as much as their commercial counterparts, the only difference being that they are not selling products but concepts, suggestions and attitudes.

Neil Postman, professor of media ecology at New York University, sees the actual commercials as modern versions of Biblical parables, in which the theme (as in the gospels) is the triumph of good over evil. 'Like all religious parables,' he says, 'they put forward a concept of sin, intimations of the way to redemption, and a vision of Heaven.' Sin in TV commercial terms means ignorance of the wonders of modern technology, redemption consists in buying the advertised product, while Heaven is (or can be if instructions on how to get there are followed without question) 'here, now, on earth, in America, and quite often in Hawaii'. A well-made TV commercial offers all the traditional trappings of religious experience, from angelic messengers to beatification and ecstasy, all in about thirty seconds. What it offers the consumer is not so much a product as an idol to be worshipped. It does so with the minimum of words and the maximum of suggestive imagery.[17]

Since the same applies to a good deal of standard television fare, it would not be surprising if viewers were influenced as much by the images of dramas, documentaries or news programmes as by those of the commercials. It is not necessary to make advertisements for suicide. This need only be presented as something that is quite easy, does not hurt much, and solves all problems. David Phillips has suggested a number of ways in which the impact of suicide stories can be lessened, such as keeping them off front pages and not mentioning the form of death in the headline. He has also found evidence of self-restraint on the part of some newspaper editors and public health officials in the publicising of suicides.

Another way the impact of a suicide story can be lessened is by presenting a 'counter-advertisement' along with it. This seems to have worked well in the fictional series devoted to the Samaritans, but television rarely has the patience to go into anything in detail and the causes of suicide can hardly be summarised at all briefly. Neil Postman recalls one news programme in which Part One of a 'special in-depth report' on depression lasted just under three minutes.[18] In-depth reports simply do not work on television. Much better are students jumping in front of trains.

A friend of mine once drove into a lamp post at Hyde Park Corner on New Year's Eve, a time when police and press give special attention to road accident figures. I went to see him in hospital.

'Oh, man,' he wailed. 'I've become a statistic!'

So he had, and in spite of what I said earlier about there being only one television statistic that really matters – there is too much of it – I make no apology for emphasising statistics in this chapter. They do have their uses, although these are strictly limited. People who crash cars or kill themselves automatically become statistics, yet the figures can only tell us what has actually happened. They cannot tell us how people are feeling or thinking. We do not see headlines in the papers like WAVE OF INFANT HYPERACTIVITY HITS PAINSWICK or TEENAGE BOREDOM INCREASES, SHOCK REPORT REVEALS. Yet people who are hyperactive or bored can affect others in many unpleasant ways, perhaps doing as much damage to society in the long run as people who become statistics.

That said, it cannot be denied that the suicide statistics mentioned provide some of the best evidence we have that a televised image can provoke an extreme act of violence. If it can do this, what else can it do? Is it not likely that any image at all is the potential cause of an action, good or bad? If this were not so, why bother to make commercials and spend millions to have them screened? This is one argument the TV lobby always tries to avoid. The evidence that television advertising hugely increases sales of absolutely anything is overwhelming. It does this occasionally by straightforward presentation of fact, but more often in the form of image-parables made with skill by leading film directors, whose services do not come cheap. With sufficient repetition, results are guaranteed, and there is plenty of evidence that

TV advertising has some effect the first time it is shown. It follows that any kind of image-parable will have some effect whether its message is explicitly spelled out or not.

Students at TV charm schools learn at least four standard defences against evidence that does not suit their cause:

1. 'Ah, but the experts don't agree.' This is undeniable, and should always be countered with, 'They never agree about anything.' Experts do not become experts by agreeing with what their colleagues say, but by tearing it to pieces. Scientific research is a rough business, in which the struggle for supremacy sometimes resembles that of trees in the rainforest. It is time this excuse was given a rest.

2. 'Yes, but doubts have been cast on so-and-so's research.' This is a more insidious version of the previous point. It is harder to deal with, tends to become rather personal, and sometimes ends in libel actions. Doubting the research of others is quite proper, but there are limits. Nobody is perfect, including both scientists and their critics. Eysenck and Nias cite the case of a 1975 report from a University of Leicester team that absolved the mass media from responsibility for any significant effect on the level of violence in society – just what the TV lobby wanted to hear. They reached this conclusion by finding something wrong with every study that had reported findings unfavourable to the media. To insist on perfection in scientific research, say Eysenck and Nias, is to ensure that 'no conclusion can ever be reached'.[19] Which suits the TV lobby perfectly. This ploy was used with brazen aplomb by the narrator of the film already mentioned in which I became involved. A brief and dismissive reference to former Cambridge parapsychologist Carl Sargent in the form of an unsupported allegation was made, in true flat-earth TV tradition, to seem equal to the combined testimony of the several hundred people (including me) who had taken part in Sargent's laboratory experiments. None of this testimony, of course, was mentioned.

3. 'More research is needed before we can reach a conclusion.' This is usually true of just about anything, and it
is a very useful ploy for getting out of tight corners. I have
given several examples of research that is crying out for
replication, such as the brain-wave studies of Mulholland
and Krugman, and of necessary research that has not
been done, such as a global survey of TV ownership and
increase in violence. However, conclusions can be reached
on the basis of very little evidence, as in the cases of the
effects of lead on the brain and of the suddenly fashionable
'greenhouse effect'. The anti-lead campaign was an aston-
ishingly short and successful one. In Britain, it owed much
to the work of a single scientist, Professor Derek Bryce-
Smith of Reading University, and an exceptionally skilled
environmental lobbyist, Des Wilson. The motor industry
began to go lead-free almost overnight. The greenhouse
effect suddenly caught the public imagination in the late
1980s, long after it was first described (it is mentioned in
my 1970 *American Heritage Dictionary* and I wrote about it
in my book, *The Cycles of Heaven*, published in 1978). This
was probably partly due to the widely publicised destruction
of the Amazon rainforest (I first wrote about that in 1973)
and Mrs Thatcher's surprising discovery after nearly ten
years in power that there was a potential global environmental problem.

We heard little about 'the need for more research' into
either lead or the effects of fossil fuels and CFC gases on
the ozonosphere. Both official and public opinions were
formed without much of a scientific base in comparison
with most fields of research. Perhaps we were lucky that
the essential features of both are fairly easy to understand:
lead upsets our neurotransmitters and affects behaviour by
direct interference with body chemistry, while an altered
ozone layer interferes with the natural exchange of energy
between sun and earth, at least in theory.

Television's effects are just as harmful as those of lead
or CFC gases, and a great deal more widespread. Yet
concepts of what it actually does to people are harder to

grasp, and there has yet to be a sudden revision in the public's viewing habits. The day will come, however, when existing research findings reach a kind of critical mass that will trigger a sudden change of attitude. There is already just as much evidence, if not more, for the damage being done by television as for damage caused by lead or aerosol sprays, but television covers its tracks by driving viewers' brains into a state in which they cannot register what is being done to them, so the build-up of that critical mass will be a long and slow one. Its eventual explosion should be dramatic.

4. 'Our research indicates . . .' Finally, we come to the most devious defence ploy of all. It consists in setting up a research project designed to give whatever result best suits the researcher or sponsor. It is standard practice in the electricity industry, which pours out a stream of research papers proving that electrical and magnetic fields have no effects at all on people while those unfortunate enough to live near power lines continue to experience a wide range of side-effects ranging from headaches to sudden death.

Fake research can be carried out by honest scientists with the best of intentions. The NBC-sponsored suicide survey mentioned earlier may have been an example of this. It might have seemed sensible to a conscientious researcher to collect data for every single suicide reported, and the person responsible may not have read Phillips' work carefully enough to know that only widely publicised cases have any effect. Unfortunately, such negative findings tend to be used to imply that earlier positive findings have been disproved. They can even be used to denigrate subsequent research as in the case of the famous Himmelweit report of 1958, which was still being used for this purpose thirty years later.

More research is undoubtedly needed, but it must be genuine and not the kind of non-research sponsored by the television industry in which experiments are designed, whether deliberately or unconsciously, to produce the results it wants. The industry has sponsored a great deal of research in the past, some of which has been mentioned, and some of which was genuinely useful such as the Belson survey of children and violence and the brain-wave studies of Herbert Krugman of General Electric. Other research, like the IBA report that found people to be different, is useless. The industry is never likely to undertake research that could undermine its reasons for existence.

Such research must therefore be done without involvement or interference of any kind from the TV industry or lobby. A huge research programme could be funded overnight simply by adding £1 to the television licence fee. Once this was under way, I suspect that at last the experts would start to agree.

PART FOUR

The whole climate of thought will be
different. In fact there will *be* no thought, as
we understand it now. Orthodoxy is
unconsciousness.

George Orwell, *Nineteen Eighty-Four*

After those weeks of idleness in London, with
nothing to do, whenever he wanted anything,
but to press a switch or turn a handle, it was
pure delight to be doing something that
demanded skill and patience.

Aldous Huxley, *Brave New World*

11

WELCOME TO NOTEL

The town of Notel (population 2,500) is not to be found on any map of Canada. Yet it does exist under another name, and it was there that a unique study of the influence of television was carried out. The story of how it came about began with the publication in 1972 of the US Surgeon General's report (mentioned earlier), claimed by Surgeon General Sternfeld himself to be the first to establish the causal link between TV and antisocial behaviour. Psychologist Tannis MacBeth Williams of the University of British Columbia thought, after reading the report, what a pity it was that before-and-after studies of television's effects on whole communities could no longer be done, for the simple reason that there were no more 'before' communities of any size left in North America. Or so she assumed.

A year later, she learned that she was wrong. There was a TV-free community in Canada and it was quite accessible, though for some geographical reason it had not yet been reached by either the Canadian Broadcasting Corporation (CBC) or the American networks that most of southern Canada had been receiving for many years. It sounded like just what she wanted, but she had to move quickly: progress was on the way and Notel, as she called the place, was due to be hooked up to CBC about a year later.

She moved quickly, locating 'control' towns in the area that were similar except for their television consumption. One was receiving four channels from Canada and the

USA while the other could get only CBC. She called them Multitel and Unitel respectively. Then she and a team of colleagues set out to find what differences, if any, there were between residents of the three communities, using a wide range of standard psychological tests on groups of both adults and children.

One of her first findings was completely unexpected: Notel adults were a good deal brighter than those of the other two towns. They were much better at creative problem-solving tests, and even those individuals who were unable to solve the tasks they were given would try for much longer than Multitel or Unitel people before giving up. As for the children of Notel, they came out at the top of the three-town league when they were given the Alternate Uses Task, a standard test in which subjects are asked how many things they can do with something, like a sheet of newspaper. This is a more revealing test than it may sound for it points to what psychologists call ideational fluency, or the ability to form ideas and mental images, and it is considered to be a good indicator of overall creativity and ability to think properly.

The Notel youngsters did not come out top in all tests, however. In one they came last – that which tested them for aggression. It soon became clear to Dr Williams that both the young and old of Notel were making much better use of their brains than their counterparts in the other two towns, but she could not prove that this was entirely due to their TV-free lives, whatever she might have suspected. It could be that Notel had better teachers, or there could be some obscure factor that she had not been able to identify. So, having at least established that there were significant differences between the people of Notel and those of the other two towns, she went away and came back two years later (by which time Notel had been receiving CBC television for a year) to see if anything had changed.

It certainly had. The first thing she noticed was 'a dramatic drop' in community participation. People were not going to public dances, parties and suppers, club meetings, concerts, parades or bingo nights as they had when there was no TV in their homes. This applied to all age levels, but was 'particularly striking' among the older people. As for the young ones, on re-testing the same children she had tested two years previously for aggression, Dr Williams was startled to find that instead of being bottom of the league they were now top, thanks to a sharp increase in both verbal and physical aggression. Moreover, this did not apply only to those who had been aggressive by nature to start with, but to the whole lot.

Their reading skills had suffered, too. Whereas in the old days, without TV, the poor readers had tended to try harder and practise, acquisition rates of reading skills in Notel had slowed down to what had to be considered normal in the tele-saturation age. Dr Williams suspected that television was encouraging young people to accept ready-made ideas and thus become 'mentally passive'. It also seemed to have led to a loss of individual personality and the adoption of 'stereotype' attitudes, the word meaning in this context somebody who is 'considered to typify or conform to an unvarying pattern or manner, lacking any individuality' (*American Heritage Dictionary*). Television, she noted, tended to portray men and women as stereotypes with the result that viewers' attitudes had become more standardised. This is a good example of an effect of television that receives far less attention than violence, but may be just as damaging to society in the long run. Television naturally gives priority to negative and destructive stereotypes, from strikers, pickets and football hooligans to political or religious fanatics and extremists. These are good television. Once a stereotype is established, individuals will conform to it in increasing numbers as a result of the processes mentioned earlier (subliminal image-absorption, post-hypnotic indirect suggestion) and behave in the way in which they have come to be expected to behave. Thus a mass stereotype is created, greatly helped by the 'mental passivity' induced by looking at images. When reading or listening to radio we remain fully active mentally: as we mix the words we see or hear with the images they inspire. When watching television we are mentally passive. On goes the set, off goes the mind and in comes the stereotype to shape our future thoughts and actions.

Dr Williams concluded that 'the net effects of North American television on regular viewers, especially children, are negative.' Why then, it will be asked, did earlier researchers reach other conclusions? Wilbur Schramm, who did a before-and-after study in Canada a few years after the Himmelweit study in Britain, reached conclusions similar to hers: not much difference and nothing to get excited about. What was so different about the Williams survey?

There are two answers. It was a good deal more thorough – Dr Williams's final report runs to 446 pages of small print packed with first-hand observations and measurements[1] – and she and her predecessors were not comparing the same things at all. Neither Schramm nor Himmelweit could use control groups of lifelong viewers because in those days there were none. The Notel study was unique because it was able to do this, and also to record individual changes of personality and behaviour at first hand.

It may never be possible to repeat the Notel study anywhere outside the Third World, but we can still compare the relative effects of light and heavy viewing, which is the next best thing. Some recent studies of this kind lend strong support to the view that television's net effect is negative. In 1986, a group of psychologists at Murdoch University in Western Australia assessed the imaginative abilities of 291 ten- to thirteen-year-olds in relation to the number of hours they spent every week watching television. Unless there is a misprint in the report, some of them were glued to their boxes for a staggering fifty hours a week, *or more*. Not surprisingly, this 'heavy viewing' group scored lower on imaginative problem-solving tests than either moderate or light viewers. Results, say the researchers, were consistent with previous studies that had shown heavy viewing to have suppressed younger children's imaginative play.[2]

The imagination is not all that suffers. Dr Larry Tucker, a community health worker from Auburn, Alabama, looked at the mental and physical health of 406 teenage boys in comparison with their viewing habits and came to a very clear conclusion: 'The well-being of the boys was related significantly to the extent of television viewing.' He reeled off a list of qualities he found in the light viewing group: 'More physically fit, emotionally stable, sensitive, imaginative, outgoing, physically active, self-controlled, intelligent, moralistic, college-bound, church-oriented and self confident than their counterparts, especially heavy television viewers.' Tucker also found the light viewers less likely to be using drugs than moderate or especially heavy viewers.[3]

An even more forthright conclusion was reached by California's state school superintendent after a large-scale survey in 1980 of the relative academic achievement and viewing habits of some half a million pupils. 'Television', he stated, 'is not an asset and ought to be turned off.'[4]

Some of the best evidence in support of this statement has been put together by writer Marie Winn in the course of her extensive research into the effects of TV on children. Taking the year 1964 as a base, she looked at the national average scores for the Scholastic Aptitude Test (SAT) between then and 1981. This test is taken by American high school students before they go on to college, and it contains an oral section in which reasoning skills can be evaluated. In 1964, when America's first generation raised on TV was ready to take the SAT, the average score for this section was 478 out of a maximum of 800. Twenty years later it was down to 424, a drop of 11 per cent. Scores of 600 or more are considered to show what an official calls 'a higher order of reasoning skills', and there had been a corresponding drop in this group from 11 to 7 per cent over the period from 1972 to 1982. What made it likely that viewing habits had something to do with this was the fact that the long and gradual decline in SAT scores matched the long and gradual increase in daily viewing hours for the same age group, notably among the brighter students.[5]

Evidence like this alone does not prove that TV makes children stupid. It could be that clever ones are less inclined to watch the thing, or there could be a third factor that causes both academic brilliance and allergy to the box. Statistical correlations are only of any value when there is a cause-and-effect theory that has been demonstrated to go with them. It is not enough to show that stupid youths watch more television. What needs explaining is why they may be stupid because they watch it.

One of the most revealing experiments involving any aspect of television was carried out in the early '80s by a Harvard University research group who set out to compare ways in which children respond to what they read in a book and what they see on the TV screen. They did this by presenting exactly the same material to two groups of children: one group simply had to sit and listen to somebody reading them a story while the other group was shown a specially made film in which the same story was read while illustrations from the book were shown on the screen. The real-life story-teller and the TV narrator were the same person. In fact everything was the same except the means by which information was conveyed.

Results, however, were not the same at all. When the two groups were tested afterwards, the book group was found to have taken in a good deal more of the story than the TV group. They could recall whole chunks of it verbatim as well as several details, whereas the TV group showed that they had absorbed the images to a far greater extent than the words, accepting them as what the project director described as 'a self-contained experience' unrelated to their own real-life experience. Children in the book group were also much better than those in the telly group when it came to discussing the story. This experiment, which would be very easy to repeat, is of special interest because it shows that it is not so much the content of a TV programme that affects viewers negatively as the medium itself. By suppressing 'inferential reasoning', creative thought becomes impossible, and it could well be argued that a society deprived of creative thought is in just as bad a way as one beset by violent behaviour.[6]

Another way in which television affects everybody is almost too obvious to mention, yet in the case of small children it may be the most influential of all. This is what psychologists call displacement, which simply means that if one is doing something, one is not doing something else. There are people who claim to be able to watch TV and do something else at the same time; in the survey by Taylor and Mullan mentioned earlier one woman said she always had the set on while she was doing her ironing. I am glad she does not do mine. For the most part, however, television displaces a great deal that used to be thought necessary for the normal development of a child from reading, playing, making things, talking to others and generally finding out how the real world works.

What does it provide in return, other than peace and quiet for parents? It offers totally artificial experience with which children cannot interact except by pressing a button and switching to another equally artificial experience. It presents a world in which value judgment is impossible since everything and everybody in it are dished up in exactly the same shape and size, adding yet more isolated images to the child's mental store of unprocessed information. It teaches instant gratification, which children learn to expect on demand in the real world. It displaces what Marie Winn calls the 'special quality that distinguishes one family from another' that largely depends on 'what a family *does*' (her emphasis). It displaces all those little bits and pieces of shared experience that become our most precious memories, turning the family into no more than what she calls 'a caretaking institution'.[7]

It also makes you fat. Two paediatricians from Tufts University in Boston have produced evidence that obesity and television viewing are causally related. Going through data provided by the US National Health and Examination Survey, they discovered a correlation between the time adolescents spent in front of the box and the probability of their developing obesity.[8] Why this is so is not too hard to imagine. In a sampling of television commercials, G. M. Blythe, director of the Oxford Health Education Unit, found that 14 per cent promoted cake, biscuits, chocolate, potato crisps and similar snacks, often accompanied by such slogans as 'Are you getting enough?' or 'If you like a lot of . . .' Pearl Coleman, the therapist mentioned earlier, has given a vivid account of the effect of a 'high television diet' on her well-nourished teenage son, whose normal weekly viewing was a mere three to four hours a week. Then a friend went on holiday and lent him his portable TV set.

On the first night of his unfamiliar high-TV diet, the boy 'announced from his bedroom in a loud voice that he was "peckish, hungry, famished and starving" in that order'. As the week wore on, 'the week's supply of fruit disappeared from the fruit bowls, refilled many times from the larder, the dried fruit and nut jars . . . emptied rapidly. Boxes of wholewheat cereal disappeared.' By the end of the week, the lad had gained half a stone.[9]

Television seems likely to be causing far more damage than this. Larry Tucker, the community worker mentioned earlier, was not the first to notice a link between watching television and taking drugs. This was discussed at length by Milton Shulman, who suggested five different reasons why the sharp increase in illegal drug consumption that took place in the USA, Canada and Britain during the '60s could be associated with TV-viewing habits in those countries, all of which reached the 90 per cent home ownership level at that time.

First was defiance of authority, actively encouraged by television and all too easy to express by experimenting with illegal drugs such as LSD-25 and cannabis. (LSD-25 was made illegal in 1966.) Second was the question of frustrated rising expectations and the rejection of the materialism tirelessly promoted on the TV screen from which mind-altering substances offered the easiest escape. Third, and perhaps the most important, was what Shulman called 'the dream imperative', by which TV had created such an insatiable need for visual stimulation that the transition to drugs of the hallucinogenic kind was only to be expected. Fourth was what a Canadian sociologist called 'stimulus flooding and psychological numbing', largely caused by TV-watching and leading in turn to drug-taking as a kind of self-defence. Finally, Shulman noted the similarities between the TV-watching experience and the narcotic vision. I have already mentioned that the former can be a narcotic addiction in itself, and it is well known that one addiction often leads to or is replaced by another.[10]

Was it just a coincidence that between 1964 and 1968, when America's first TV generation came of age, the proportion of teenagers among those arrested for drug offences doubled? On the evidence from some of the addicts themselves collected by Marie Winn, I would guess not. One described the effects of cannabis as being like 'a TV show', another mentioned watching acid-induced imagery 'like on a TV show', while a third showed some sign of increased perceptivity by noting that one effect of drug-taking was to blur the line between the real and the unreal, adding: 'Just like with TV'. It is hardly surprising that drug-takers make use of such television-inspired metaphors as turning on and tuning in, or that having done so both drug and TV addicts 'drop out'.[11]

Not only does television deprive viewers of more than it gives them, but what it does give them is almost always something they either have already or could have with the minimum of effort. How many devotees of the much praised nature series *The Living Planet* know that the armadillo, the giant ant-eater, and some of the fish, snakes and rodents used in early episodes were borrowed for the occasion from a zoo, which was presumably open to the public?[12] I also wonder what prompted David Attenborough, who made the series, to say this when he left his job as head of BBC television programming: 'One of the things that worries me, which you can't very well say if you are a Director of Programmes, is that people watch television too much.' He said it on television, too. Good for him.[13]

An often heard defence of TV is that it encourages people to turn to real pursuits such as sports, hobbies, or sciences like astronomy. Laurie Taylor and Bob Mullan go so far as to claim that 'the whole area of ecology and conservationism generally has been enormously helped by television'.[14] The first argument is an unusual one – if the best thing television can do is to encourage people to do something other than watch it, usually something that people have been doing since long before TV was invented, I can only wonder why there was any need to watch the thing in the first place.

The second one is equally questionable. Television has certainly jumped on to the green bandwagon, but it has merely hijacked a cause pioneered over many years by such groups as Friends of the Earth, Greenpeace, and the European Green parties, especially the West German one. The result, says critic Fred Pearce, has been 'too many hurriedly produced programmes, commissioned by people who have only the vaguest idea of what they want, and made by producers and researchers with too little knowledge and too little time to acquire it'. A film on the destruction of the Amazon rainforest, for example, offered 'apocalyptic quotes and pictures of sunsets in place of explanation of how destroying trees could warm the planet'. TV is good at covering ecological disasters, he says, but unless it learns 'how to present the bigger but less photogenic and less sudden disasters' the result will be, as environmental consultant Chris Rose puts it, 'like covering economics by only covering bank robberies'.[15]

There are always special cases, and television's is *The*

Sky At Night. Who would have dared imagine in the late 1940s that the BBC's longest running programme would be devoted entirely to astronomy, and would be presented by the same man for something like half a century? Increased interest in this science, according to Taylor and Mullan, was due 'almost single-handedly' to Patrick Moore. Now, Moore is both a real astronomer of distinction and a natural communicator whose programmes I remember fondly. I cannot hear the opening bars of Sibelius's *Pelléas et Mélissande* without automatically looking heavenwards to see where the stars are. Yet people have been doing this since the dawn of recorded history. Astronomy has always been the most popular of the sciences, and amateurs have made major contributions to it. Sir William Herschel, trained as a musician, discovered the planet Uranus. Graham Hosty, trained as a postman, found a new star (Nova Sagitta 1977) with defective equipment worth about £10. If Patrick Moore has increased popular interest in astronomy in the TV age, so much the better. Yet television did not invent it. Indeed, if television had never been invented, astronomy might be even more popular than it is even after forty years of *The Sky at Night*. There would be a lot more time for star-gazing.

If something is to be criticised, it should be criticised at its best as well as its worst. So I carried out an opinion poll among my televiewing friends, who came up with two almost unanimous nominations for television's finest hour: the news reports from Ethiopia that led to the Band Aid phenomenon, and the film *Cathy Come Home*. This film, which I did manage to see, was undoubtedly a masterpiece. Jeremy Sandford's story about the plight of homeless people was researched at first hand, and Kenneth Loach's direction transformed it into a film that was more realistic than any documentary. Yet although it deservedly won several prizes and even led to changes in the law, what good did it do in the long run? According to the author himself, the number of people in hostels for the homeless went up from 12,411 in 1966 (the year in which the film was first shown) to 32,292 ten years later. Local authority waiting-lists had swelled over the same period from 150,000 to 238,000.[16] In 1989 there were an estimated 75,000 homeless in London alone. Cathy had still not come home.

I did not see the material from Ethiopia that inspired the singer Bob Geldof to 'get off my backside and do something about it,' as he put it in the moving radio interview which I did hear. Indeed, I had no need to see the images of famine and dying children since Geldof described them so vividly, reminding me what a great visual medium radio can be. What he did after getting off his backside was to raise something like £50 million almost overnight, and mobilise what seemed to be the entire worldwide entertainment profession in an extraordinary feat of organisation that soon had plane loads of food and supplies on their way to Ethiopia. Having myself worked in the foreign aid business for four years, I could not fail to be impressed.

However, three years later there was still famine in Ethiopia. The first thing I learned when I went to work for the US Agency for International Development in Brazil was the house motto: 'Give a man a fish, and you feed him for a day. Teach a man to fish, and you feed him for the rest of his days.' The next thing I learned was that problems are not solved by money alone. If they were, the developed world would not have any. They are solved by removing the cause of the problem, which cannot be done overnight even by revolutionary governments such as those of Cuba or Nicaragua. To change anything it is sometimes necessary to change everything.

To find out why people in Britain have nowhere to live or why Ethiopians have nothing to eat involves tedious examination of many subjects, from political and social structures to local industry and climate. This kind of enquiry does not make for good television. Cathy wandering the streets and African children starving to death are much better, and television, in the long run, did little for either. It merely exploited them for its own purposes. The former BBC sports presenter David Icke, who is also a national speaker for the Green Party, admits: 'We must move our approach in the media from the purely environmental (symptoms) to the truly green (cause and effect).'[17]

He may find this difficult, for television typifies the kind of technological dictatorship that Greens aim to abolish. It can indeed transform society, as the Notel study showed, but it does not solve its problems. It just transmutes them into yet more entertainment.

IS THERE LIFE AFTER
TELEVISION?

The idea of giving up television for good is seldom tak-
en very seriously. Here, for example, is the opinion of a
television critic:

> It is an absurd middle-class fantasy to imagine that if
> only people could be induced to turn their televisions
> off they would all start reading Solzhenitsyn and going
> to Covent Garden or attending lectures on the Late
> Renaissance.[1]

Is it though? We are not told on what evidence this
opinion is based. There is plenty of evidence for life after
television, and to find out what people really do when they
turn off their sets, why not ask them?

In 1971 a group of West German psychologists offered
to pay people a weekly fee if they gave up their viewing
habit for a year. A total of 184 regular viewers agreed to
take part in the experiment, and once they had turned their
sets off it was found that they went out to the cinema three
times as often as before, visited friends and relatives twice
as often, and doubled the time they spent reading or playing
games. Ninety-three per cent reported taking more interest
in their children's affairs.

Yet this particular experiment was a failure. There were
reports of an increase in domestic strife and even physical
violence. Dramatic effects on couples' sex lives were also
noted, with husbands less inclined to make love to their

wives but more inclined to have affairs. The first volunteer to drop out did so after only three weeks, and not one stayed the full year's course. In fact, none survived even half of it. All were back in front of their screens within five months. Psychologist Henner Ertel commented: 'With people who watch regularly, many behaviour patterns become so closely related to TV that they are negatively influenced if one takes the set away. The problem is that of addiction.'[2]

In 1974 the *Denver Post* appealed for volunteers with small children to take part in a similar experiment for at least a month. Twenty-five families accepted the challenge and fifteen survived the full month. Although run by a newspaper and not a scientist, this was actually a very useful experimental field study, much better documented than others of its type. Participants were given a detailed questionnaire beforehand together with hints on how to soften the blow to children when sets were switched off. They were also given diaries in which to record changes in behaviour.

Even before the experimental period some interesting facts came to light. Asked why they had volunteered, parents painted a depressing picture of their home lives, clearly identifying television as a displacer of other activities. One wanted 'to have the children explore other ways of entertaining themselves'. Another hoped they would find out 'how many more exciting things there are to do'. A third wanted 'to help our family discover alternative forms of time-structuring'. There were familiar complaints that TV was taking over their lives, making it impossible to communicate with each other or just wasting time. One desperate parent admitted to using television 'as a substitute for everything'. How's that for displacement?

The Denver experiment produced some highly positive results. Although there were difficult transition periods in some cases, benefits reported ranged from greatly increased family togetherness and interaction and a sharp increase in time spent reading to a wider range of activities for both parents and children. There was a sudden outbreak of creativity among the latter described by one parent as 'real old-fashioned playing'. Even so, when the month was up all the Denver families switched on again. One perceptive child later recalled, 'I had more fun. I had to kick the habit.'[3]

To judge from these experiments, and another in Britain organised by the *Daily Mirror* in 1984, in which only 3 out of 42 families managed to survive without TV for just a week, sudden forced abstinence is not the best way to escape from the clutches of television. A better one, it seems, is to go and live somewhere like Notel where there isn't any. This may be difficult today anywhere in the developed world, but it was still possible in Colorado in 1971 when the Lee family and their three small children went to live in a place called Vail. The children, according to their mother, were all 'TV addicts' but they were forced to go cold turkey on arrival because Vail was beyond the reach of Cable Vision and a mountain was jamming all other network signals.

Whatever did the Lees do out there in the sticks? They read books, played records, entertained friends, taught the children to play draughts and generally had a pretty good time. Mrs Lee did some 'serious' sewing and increased her cooking repertoire. 'There just seemed to be more time in a day,' she recalled later. As for the children, they devised enough play activities to keep themselves happy indoors or out. Then after two and a half years without TV the Lees moved to an urban apartment block where there were no play facilities. Back came the set, and the children were up at 7 a.m. to watch yet another rerun of *Lassie* or *The Lone Ranger*. Life went back to normal.

If enforced separation from the box does not seem to work once the service is available again, how about voluntary deprivation for an experimental period? This was tried by a New York policeman as part of his sociology course. He fixed both the sets in his house so that they would not work and settled down to see what would happen. After a shaky start the effects were beneficial. The children (aged five and six), who had been watching forty or more hours a week, worked out some creative activities for themselves while their mother had a good spring-clean and sewed a couple of dresses. The family worked together in their garden and went out three times to visit friends. Then the two-week experiment ended and 'everything reverted back to its old routine'.[4]

Marie Winn, who has collected some of the best evidence on life without television, including the above cases, asked a psychologist why it was that experiments such as these so often had only temporary effects. His view was that people had been deceiving themselves into thinking they were better off reading, playing around or just talking to each other, but had found that such activities just did not 'fulfil the needs that television viewing did'. What needs, Marie Winn wondered? The only needs she could think of that television fulfilled were for 'passivity, for self-annihilation, for regression to a state of dependence'. She wondered if the very idea of an active and creative life was becoming too much to contemplate.[5]

Here, surely, is the core of the problem? With the obvious exception of the Open University, television is nothing but entertainment. It fulfils no other needs at all and a great many people instinctively know this. Why else would they speak so often of their viewing habit as if they knew it was not doing them any good? Why does the terminology of narcotic addiction turn up again and again when people talk about it? Could it not be that it is because television is nothing more than a pointless and destructive addiction masquerading as entertainment, offering nothing positive that cannot be had without it?

I am not impressed by arguments that television has led to an increase in jogging, ballroom dancing, snooker, astronomy or whatever. It may be true that some people have at last felt the need to get away from their wretched screens now and then and do something real. If so, I cannot help wondering why television viewing has also led to an increase in television viewing?

✷

There would seem to be only three ways in which television addicts can be brought back into the real world:

1. They can be suddenly deprived of it by accident.
2. They can move to an area where TV cannot be received.
3. They can make a conscious decision to give it up.

In her search for families who were living television-free lives, Marie Winn managed to locate thirteen of them including examples of each category. The Davis family, from a rural part of New York state, lost their service when a storm broke their aerial which they could not afford to replace immediately. The parents were in any case 'fed up' with all the television they and their four children were watching, Mrs Davis reckoning that they were 'pretty addicted'. (That word yet again.) They took this chance to get TV out of their lives for good, and two years later they were a different family. The children had found all kinds of new interests and even came to feel sorry for their friends who seemed to have nothing better to do than stare at images.

The Warners won their freedom the easy way by spending six months in a part of Africa not yet colonised by television. Mrs Warner described her boys as (pardon the repetition) 'really addicted' before the trip, yet they adapted quickly and the family developed a togetherness in Africa they had never known in Pittsburgh. When the time came to go home, they resolved to keep it and they did.

The third method was used successfully by the Gerber family from New York, whose teenage son was such a hopeless case that he would sit and stare at the screen for six to seven hours non-stop. After a taste of real life on a two-month holiday, they decided to go TV-free. They did not dispose of their set, but stored it away to be brought out for special occasions – surely the ultimate test of self-control?

Of the thirteen families Marie Winn interviewed not one member, parent or child, showed any sign of wanting to relapse. True, some had problems, the most serious of which was finding a babysitter able to get through a whole evening without a TV screen to look at. Also, parents could no longer use TV deprivation as a form of punishment. Some had to get used to accusations that they were 'culturally depriving' their children. Yet the benefits of getting rid of what one parent called the 'built-in separator' that isolated family members from each other were enough to outweigh the drawbacks. Life was simply better: there was more to do and more time in which to do it.[6]

Are these abstainers merely a bunch of obstinate eccentrics like the 'book people' in Ray Bradbury's *Fahrenheit 451*, who keep banned literature alive by learning their favourite works by heart? New York University media ecologist Neil Postman thinks not. He sees them as members of a new monastic order, deliberately resisting the spirit of the age so as to preserve humane traditions and first and foremost to give children back their childhood. He compares the technological takeover of culture in this century with the takeover by the printed word that signalled its birth in the fifteenth century, emphasising the fact that whereas the Gutenberg revolution created a culture, twentieth-century technology has destroyed one.

Before Gutenberg and the introduction of printing there was nothing for most people to read, so information could only be conveyed orally. Social literacy had been unknown for a thousand years, following the fall of the Roman Empire with its precise language and rich literature. So had childhood as we know it today. The young were considered to be adults at the age of seven, when they had learned to speak fluently. There was not much else to learn, hence no schools except for a tiny minority, and no formal education other than direct experience of a very limited world. The printed book changed all that.

With the rapid growth of the school system from around 1500, children emerged as a separate group, acquiring privileges they had not known before and being treated with considerably more care and affection. No more medieval egalitarianism for them, with free access to the more ribald aspects of life. They came to be seen as needing protection from such things as sexual abuse (considered fairly normal in precultural times) and obscenity in speech. Adulthood no longer began at seven but at least ten years later, and during this long period of adolescence it became accepted that the young could not be treated as equals until they had acquired the intellectual capacity to contribute to society as equals. Education became more and more authoritarian, with adolescent minds forced to grapple with complexities of thought and to absorb knowledge of no obvious immediate interest to them. Children may at first have gone 'unwillingly to school', yet compulsory education paid unimaginably rich dividends in the form of the host of dramatists, poets and musicians who created the great Elizabethan age of culture. Shakespeare was born barely a century after the death of Gutenberg.

The Age of Childhood lasted from the sixteenth century to the 1960s, and one of its most important features was the relationship that developed between the generations. It was a distant one by today's standards with the parent as ultimate authority in all matters and main source of all information other than that provided at school or through books provided by parent or teacher. Cinema and radio broke the parent-school monopoly of 'managed information', though only to a limited extent. Each provided easily accessible experience and entertainment that called for none of the effort involved in reading a book, and each was criticised in its time for lowering cultural standards and generally leading the young astray. Yet radio did much to stimulate creative visualisation, not only in plays and talks but also in such entertainment classics as *The Goon Show*, *Hancock's Half Hour* and the more recent *Hitchhiker's Guide to the Galaxy*. The radio listener, like the book reader, was obliged to participate. We all had our own cherished idea of what the Hancock home looked like, and it was a sad day for his fans when television tried to take over the show. The cinema has had its critics ever since it was invented, and it may be thought that objections to television should also apply to films. Two popular feature films, *Soldier Blue* and *A Clockwork Orange*, provoked widely publicised copycat crimes that led to their being banned on television, suggesting that the potentially harmful influence of imagery is well understood by the industry. Since the early 1970s the cinema has offered the public far more than television in the way of sex, violence and general depravity. Yet there are two fundamental differences between the two media. One is that the cinema offers its product on its own territory, whereas television invades the home. This is a difference of considerable psychological significance. The other, equally obvious, is that whereas television diminishes and belittles, the cinema enlarges. Film stars are a good deal larger than life especially in close-up, and we have a natural tendency to look 'up' to them just as we unconsciously look 'down' on the miniaturised world of television.

On balance the contributions to culture of both radio and the cinema have been overwhelmingly positive. Breaking the parent-school monopoly in childhood information management was not in itself a bad thing. The cinema, for all its faults, never became addictive on the scale of television. One would have to go to a cinema at least once a day every day of the year to equal the average time spent watching TV. At 1990 prices this would cost nearly twenty times the price of a colour TV licence. As for radio, while there is definitely life without television, life without radio is too dreadful to contemplate. No other medium comes anywhere near it for its combination of instant news, thorough analysis, width and depth of coverage of all cultural fields, variety of entertainment and general good fun, not to mention its unique ability to stimulate the waking brain instead of sending it to sleep.

Television has upset the balance of the family in a way that the cinema and the radio never did. As Neil Postman points out, watching it neither requires nor develops any skills at all. Unlike reading, it can be done without learning. Nobody has to teach us to see, and the simple act of looking at something makes no demands on the intellect. Moreover, while in Shakespeare's day there may have been seven ages of man, in the television age there are only three: infancy, senility, and everything in between. In these ways, Postman explains, television has brought back the world of the Dark Ages in which there was no real distinction made between child and adult and when it could be said that 'everything is for everybody'.

It is all very well to provide innocuous cartoons at teatime for the tots and keep up the pretence that all children are tucked up in bed by 9 p.m., but the facts prove otherwise. According to Postman, 3 million American children aged 2 to 11 are still up at 11.30 p.m., more than a million of them after midnight, doing guess what? It is doubtful that any small child would get beyond the first paragraph of *Finnegan's Wake*, but children of any age can look at any kind of television or video material, and as we know they do. If children have unlimited access to adult information, is it surprising that they gradually turn into miniature adults?

Thus we now have boys of 12 in three-piece suits, girls of 11 in high heels, and Olympic medallists who retire, already over the hill, at 18 after being professionalised out of their natural lives and force-trained into precocious champions. We have teenage bank robbers, drug addicts, rapists and – increasingly – alcoholics. At the 1989 conference of the Institute of Alcohol Studies, results were announced of a survey of the drinking habits of 33,000 children aged 11 to 15. It was found that more than half of the 11-year-olds were averaging four units of alcohol a week (the equivalent of two pints of beer or four glasses of wine or spirits), with more than three quarters of the 15-year-olds getting through an average of 11 units. Many of the children had begun drinking before the age of 11, and alcohol was named as 'a major factor in promoting school violence, truancy and classroom disruption'.[7]

At about the same time, Essex county probation officer Alan Critchley was describing the spectacular drinking habits of some of his customers in the 17 to 20 age group, who were getting through no less than 120 pints of strong lager a week; about three times the maximum considered safe for adults. Mr Critchley described his findings, somewhat unfortunately, as 'sobering'. Meanwhile, up in the North, the Northern Regional Health Authority discovered that a quarter of all 16 to 20-year-olds were classified as heavy drinkers, with a weekly consumption of 24 or more units. More than a quarter of these admitted to having been involved in fights after drinking.[8] Lager seems to be the youthful boozer's favourite, especially the extra-strength variety brewed in Denmark (and known there as Easter Brew because it is not allowed to be sold at any other time). By an amazing coincidence, lager is one of the most heavily advertised of all products on British television. In Sweden, by contrast, there was a 20 per cent drop in per capita alcohol consumption when TV commercials for it were banned.[9]

With a steady stream of information pouring into the home on everything from sex, pregnancy, alcohol and drugs to venereal disease and AIDS, who needs parents or schoolteachers? There is nothing left for them to teach, at least nothing children are interested in learning from them. Parents and teachers are becoming increasingly redundant. The result of this great leap backwards in cultural evolution has meant that it is becoming increasingly difficult to tell an adult from a child. They look alike, dress alike, speak alike and share the same attitudes and desires. Children have indeed become, in Postman's phrase, 'an endangered species'.

Some of them, it seems, no longer learn very much. A shopkeeper in prosperous Brighton advertised for a counter assistant and received thirteen applicants of school-leaving age. He gave them all a test in which they were asked to work out the cost of a £25.65 suit-case, two £1.60 spectacle cases and a £5.75 manicure set less a 10 per cent discount. They were given pencil, paper and all the time they wanted, but even so eight of them got the wrong answer. A local education spokesman came out with this reassuring comment: 'There has always been difficulty for less academic youngsters to apply their mathematical skills to real-life situations.' He added that East Sussex pupils' maths results were 'generally above the national average'. For his part, the shopkeeper wanted to know why 'teaching standards seem to have dropped'.[10]

One possible reason came to light when Marie Winn visited an unnamed American high school and found the 'English' class to be entirely devoted to making videos and 'studying' television shows. The teacher explained somewhat mystifyingly that one of his prime goals was to use TV as 'a motivational tool for reading and for writing'. In what Winn calls 'an act of true desperation', American teachers now regularly assign television viewing as 'homework', knowing that their pupils are not likely to do anything else.[11]

Teachers are, it seems, also an endangered species, at least in the prosperous south-east of England where an education authority advertised for some in 1989 and received just one applicant. He turned out to be unsuitable, so the authority was eventually forced to import teachers from West Germany where there was a surplus of well-qualified ones. The young woman I heard on the radio programme in which this milestone in British education history was announced spoke English rather better than many Londoners.

Where will it all end? The answer is that much of it has ended, and to fight back against the technology that ended it is not easy. Yet this is what members of the New Monastic Order have decided to do. They are not prepared to sit back and let technology take control of their lives and their national institutions. 'We are just beginning to notice the spiritual and social debris that our technology has strewn about us,' says Neil Postman, and cleaning up the debris involves taking a firm stand against the anti-cultural values of the New Dark Age. As he sees it this resistance movement has to begin in the home, for if children are to become real children again parents have to become real parents. There are four things they have to do,

all of them very much out of fashion in the late twentieth
century:

1. Stay married. This is an act of rebellion in itself, or
as Postman puts it 'an insult to the spirit of a throwaway
culture in which continuity has little value'.
2. Spend more time with children in order to give
them the experience of kinship.
3. Oblige children to learn the disciplines of self-restraint
in behaviour and language, sexual modesty and 'delayed
gratification'.
4. Control children's access to the media.

All of this is difficult, time-consuming, expensive and
anti-social as social behaviour has come to be understood.
Postman ventures into a minefield I avoid at all costs when
he points out that the women's liberation movement, of
which he strongly approves in principle, is simply not com-
patible with 'traditional patterns of child care'.[12] Perhaps
the time has come for a children's liberation movement in
which they are set free from a technology that has done
much to deprive them of their rights, even though this
will mean restricting the liberty of their parents?

Teachers, who now spend more time with some children
than their parents do, are well aware of what is going on and
what has caused it. This was made clear at the meeting in
Birmingham in August 1989 of the Professional Association
of Teachers when its general secretary, former head teacher
Mr Peter Dawson, let fly at what he saw as the origin of
many of society's problems: the long-term effect of too
much television.

'Most adults have been slowly, insidiously, subconsciously rendered incapable of making balanced judgments
about right and wrong,' he said. 'That being so, how can the
next generation be expected to take any notice when they
are told to behave themselves?' He was particularly incensed
at the way teachers were being expected to clean up the mess
made by parents and other adults who no longer bothered

to 'respect authority, practise courtesy, deal honestly, live uprightly or talk cleanly'. Yet it was they who complained that children's work standards were not good enough. 'How dare they? What hypocrisy!' he stormed. 'Given the way things are, it would be absolutely astounding if young people were not disruptive, disrespectful and disobedient.'

He singled out the BBC's *EastEnders* for its 'evil influence' on society. It was 'a very good soap opera, brilliantly acted and superbly written. And that's the problem.' It projected 'as normal, highly deviant forms of behaviour' such as 'homosexuality, bad language, crime, infidelity and drunkenness' and gave the impression that this was 'what real life is like'.[13]

Members of the 42,000-strong association voted by a huge majority in favour of a motion to demand less violence on television and to ask parents to recognise its influence on their children's behaviour. One member gave a description of a recent example she had observed in which a couple of three-year-olds were imitating robots from a popular TV series aimed at their age group. One attacked the other as the robots did and seemed amazed that he had hurt his friend.

'I could not believe what I was seeing,' said primary school deputy head teacher Anne Spencer. 'The expression on that child's face said why wasn't his friend all right? On TV it doesn't matter if you hit each other, you always get regenerated. Why wasn't it happening in real life?' She referred to children's TV fare in general as 'insidious indoctrination' and concluded: 'By having these films in our homes and allowing children to see them we are saying to them that it is quite acceptable to behave in this way.'[14]

While this conference was going on, the BBC's research department released some figures that might have encouraged the teachers. Average viewing times by the 'AB' group of professional and high-earning people had fallen by 10 per cent between 1985 and 1989 to 17 hours 42 minutes. The national average was 26.5 hours a week, or about 3.8 hours a day. Still, any decline in viewing figures sounds like good news until we look at what is displacing it.[15]

If television itself is ever to be displaced it seems likely that its successor will be one of its own offspring: the video. Many of my objections to broadcast TV apply to the square screens of both the video monitor and the home recording system, yet each has its more acceptable face. The video recorder has freed viewers from the tyranny of the timetable, while home video cameras will document family life for posterity in a way still cameras never could. As for computers, their great advantage over television is that people actually do something with them other than sit and stare at them. Alvin Toffler's optimistic scenario of a new post-industrialist society based on the 'electronic cottage' rather than the office or factory has already begun to come true, though I see no sign of his promised 'demassified media'.[16]

It was not long before this brave new technology was being put to some fairly unpleasant uses other than the video nasty films already mentioned. American kids can now play a video game called *Death Race* in which the winner is the one who runs over the most pedestrians, while Israelis can amuse themselves with *Intifada* (uprising) in which players see how many Palestinians they can kill, wound or just capture. Messages that appear on the screen include 'You are dying because of burns over 95 per cent of your body', 'You are another victim of Arab terror', or – for successful anti-uprisers – 'Your country is most grateful. Keep up the good work.'[17] Not to be outdone, British toy manufacturers have produced their own racist computer games in which targets are Jews, police or other groups. These may be thought as harmless as the tin soldiers children used to play with, and it remains to be seen whether their effect is cathartic – channelling aggression into a harmless outlet – or whether they prepare players for the real thing in the streets.

Even at their best, and least violent or racist, such

171

games encourage the On/Off push-button zap mentality that is all too easily learned in the home and put into practice at school or work. They condition players to a life that is all action, excitement and highlight in which gratification is given instantly on demand, a life all too easily imitated outside the home in a whole hierarchy of contexts from pushing somebody off the pavement who happens to get in the way to knocking down an historic building to make room for yet another hotel or office, just two examples of everyday life in the smash-and-grab society television has helped to shape.

One does not have to be a reactionary to reject all this. Reactionaries oppose progress and call for a return to times past. Nothing could be more reactionary in fact than television, which suppresses personal progress by its destruction of natural learning processes and wallows in the past, promoting a cynical and spurious nostalgia in an endless stream of programmes devoted to World War II and commercials of the kind already mentioned for good old real bread and beer. The new reactionaries are those who roll on their backs, wave their paws in the air and let technology walk all over them without protest, deadened with the anaesthetic of all those 'mild distractions, gentle pleasures and sheer delights' we heard about earlier. To decide that one is going to have none of this is a gesture of forward-looking radical liberalism and not of any desire to return to the past.

It is not my aim to tell anybody what to do, and I am not going to end with a list of high-sounding proposals that have no chance of being carried out. Some of my predecessors have done this. Milton Shulman called for the setting up of a National Broadcasting Council which, if the Press Council is anything to go by, would be a total waste of time. Eysenck and Nias proposed something similar, while Mander simply stated that since television was unreformable (a point also made by Postman) it has to go altogether. This is a fine example of positive thinking, but it is not very realistic.

I have only two recommendations to offer. One, already mentioned, is for a serious research programme into all aspects of television influence to be funded by a small levy on the licence fee. This should include detailed study of people who do not watch any TV at all. The other is that every reader of this book who has a television set should try a simple experiment: unplug it for an experimental week and just see what happens. Some may find this easier than they think, especially if they take the opportunity to do something new, such as reading the works of Solzhenitsyn, which happens to be one of the things I did soon after going TV-free, or if they do something they have not done for some time, such as going to a cinema, theatre, concert, jazz club, museum or zoo, or simply painting the kitchen ceiling to the accompaniment of a radio programme. Radio is by far the best antidote to any withdrawal symptoms that may appear. It provides a far wider variety of both information and entertainment than television while stimulating the imagination instead of suppressing it. Moreover, it costs nothing.

Those who give up television may be as pleasantly surprised as I was to find that far from having been deprived of anything, they have been given something – the feeling of reward and enrichment that follows a real experience or an exercise of the imagination and stays in the mind for ever as a precious memory. They may decide that this feeling, which is denied to television viewers, is infinitely more gratifying than anything the kaleidoscope can provide and is something they are not prepared to give up.

When it comes to it, what does television provide? One of the most debilitating forms of narcotic addiction yet devised. A daily dose of hypnosis containing an abundance of direct and indirect suggestion, much of it negative and all of it absorbed subconsciously, with unpredictable consequences. A non-stop shower of subliminal messages absorbed in the same way with equally unpredictable effects on thought and behaviour. A parade of stereotypes to which

173

viewers find themselves conforming involuntarily. An endless course in desensitisation to violence and anti-social behaviour of all kinds. A 'mirror of society' which society itself reflects in turn only to be re-reflected in an infinite spiral of artificiality. A constantly changing kaleidoscope of random imagery offering more and more of the same. A means of elevating nonentities to spurious temporary fame while diminishing real celebrities and relieving them of their auras. A rearranging of reality in the name of 'good television'. A substitute for real experience that promises everything and delivers nothing but transitory entertainment that evaporates in the night. A mass conditioning machine that produces responses on a scale that would have alarmed Pavlov. A separator of families and insulator of individuals. An artificial substitute for everything real. The ultimate magic show in which nothing is what it appears to be. The modern equivalent of the Evil Eye which, in the words of a historian of witchcraft, 'could harm children simply by looking at them'.[18] The most pernicious and pervasive of all threats to the environment – and yet the only such threat that can be eliminated by the touch of a button.

Television? No thanks.

Not merely the validity of experience, but the very existence of external reality, was tacitly denied by their philosophy.

. . . complete uniformity of opinion on all subjects, now existed for the first time.

George Orwell, *Nineteen Eighty-Four*

REFERENCES

Chapter 1
1   *The Times*, 27 November 1982.
2   New York: William Morrow, 1978.

Chapter 2
1   S. Rushdie, *The Satanic Verses*. London: Viking Penguin, 1988, pp. 146, 58.
2   G. L. Playfair, 'The Influencing Machine'. *Vole* 3 (10), 1980.
3   N. McWhirter, *Ross. The story of a shared life*. London: Churchill Press, 1976, ch. 14.

Chapter 3
1   C. A. Siepmann, *Radio, Television and Society*. New York: Oxford University Press, 1950, p. 334.
2   Ibid., p. 331.
3   H. J. Eysenck, 'Television and the problem of violence'. *New Scientist* 12, pp. 606-7, 1960.
4   J. Mander, *Four Arguments for the Elimination of Television*. New York: William Morrow, 1978, pp. 341-3.
5   Ibid., p. 13.
6   J. Mander, Personal communication, 26 February 1980.
7   M. Shulman, *The Ravenous Eye*. London: Cassell, 1973.
8   M. Winn, *The Plug-In Drug. Television, children and the family*. Revised edition. New York/Harmondsworth: Viking Penguin, 1985.
9   D. Fisher, 'High-definition television: on the brink'. *Television* (Journal of the Royal Television Society) May-June 1988, pp. 113-16. C. W. Smith & A. A. Dumbreck, '3-D TV: the practical requirements'. Ibid., January-February 1988, pp. 9-16.

Chapter 4
1   P. G. Hepper, 'Fetal "soap" addiction'. The *Lancet*, 11 June 1988, pp. 1347-8.

References

2 M. Winn, *The Plug-In Drug. Television, children and the family*. Revised edition. New York/Harmondsworth: Viking Penguin, 1985, p. 12.
3 J. A. M. Meerloo, 'Television addiction and reactive apathy'. *Journal of Nervous and Mental Disease* 120, pp. 290-1, 1954.
4 L. Taylor & R. G. Mullan, *Uninvited Guests. The intimate secrets of television and radio*. London: Chatto & Windus 1986, p. 19.
5 Ibid., p. 207.
6 J. Mander, *Four Arguments for the Elimination of Television*. New York: William Morrow, 1978, pp. 158-9.
7 Taylor & Mullan, op. cit. pp. 182-3.
8 Quoted in A. Koestler, *The Act of Creation*. London: Pan, 1966, pp. 117-18.
9 Winn, op. cit., ch. 3.
10 P. A. Coleman, 'The Plug-in Drug'. *Epoch* 3 (1) pp. 2-7, 1980.

Chapter 5

1 G. Ambrose & G. Newbold, *A Handbook of Medical Hypnosis*. London: Baillière Tindall, 2nd ed. 1980, pp. 51-2.
2 J. Braid, *Neurypnology; or the Rationale of Nervous Sleep*. London: Churchill, 1843, pp. 112-13. (Punctuation altered.)
3 Ibid., p. 109.
4 *The Guardian*, 14 March 1988.
5 T. B. Mulholland, 'Training Visual Attention'. *Academic Therapy*, Fall 1974, pp. 5-17.
6 H. E. Krugman, 'Brain wave measures of media involvement', *Journal of Advertising Research* 11 (1) pp. 3-9, 1971.
7 M. Shulman, *The Ravenous Eye*. London: Cassell, 1973, p. 260.
8 F. Emery & M. Emery, *A Choice of Futures*. Leiden: Martinus Nijhoff, 1976, pp. 45-144.
9 J. Mander, *Four Arguments for the Elimination of Television*. New York: William Morrow, 1978, p. 211.
10 A. Moll, *Hypnotism*. London: Walter Scott, 1890, pp. 153-4.
11 Ibid., pp. 253-4.
12 M. Proust, *Du côté de chez Swann*. Paris: Gallimard, 1919, p. 72. My literal translation, with apologies to Proustians.
13 C. MacLeod-Morgan, 'Hypnosis is a Right-hemispheric task . . .' *Svensk Tidskrift for Hypnos* 10, pp. 84-90, 1983.
14 Shulman, op. cit., p. 201.
15 Emery & Emery, op. cit., p. 82.

References

Chapter 6

1 R. Greene, 'Subliminal Sweet Nothings', *San Francisco Chronicle*, 3 July 1986.

2 M. Loeb, 'It Takes a Super Imagination to See the Message on New "Super-Paper" '. *Wall Street Journal*, 13 August 1982.

3 J. G. Miller, 'Discrimination without awareness'. *American Journal of Psychology* 52, pp. 562-78, 1939.

4 M. L. De Fleur & R. M. Petranoff, 'A televised test of subliminal awareness'. *Public Opinion Quarterly* 23, pp. 168-80, 1959.

5 'Secret Voices. Messages that manipulate.' *Time*, 10 September 1979.

6 L. H. Silverman et al., 'Effect of subliminal stimulation of symbiotic fantasies on behavior modification treatment of obesity.' *Journal of Consulting & Clinical Psychology* 46 (3) pp. 432-41, 1978.
L. H. Silverman, 'An experimental method for the study of unconscious conflict: a progress report.' *British Journal of Medical Psychology* 48 (4) pp. 291-8, 1975.

7 F. P. Sandahl, 'The Defence Mechanism Test DMT as a selection instrument . . .' *Kungliga Krigsvetenskapsakademiens Handlingar och Tidskrift* 4, pp. 132-54, 1988.
A. Lowe, B. Hayward & T. Neuman, 'Defence mechanism and the prediction of performance'. XXIV International Congress of Psychology, Sydney, Australia, 1988.

8 N. F. Dixon, *Our Own Worst Enemy*. London: Jonathan Cape, 1987, p. 79.

9 N. F. Dixon, 'Subliminal perception and parapsychology: points of contact.' *Parapsychology Review*, May-June 1979, p. 4.

Chapter 7

1 R. Clutterbuck, *The Media and Political Violence*. London: Macmillan, 2nd ed., 1983, pp. 59-60.

2 P. Conrad, *Television. The Medium and its Manners*. London: Routledge & Kegan Paul, 1982, p. 126.

3 Clutterbuck, op. cit., p. xxxv.

4 Ibid., p. xxiii.

5 Ibid., p. xxxiv.

6 Ibid., p. xl.

7 Ibid., p. 114.

8 Ibid., p. 135.

References

9   Conrad, op. cit., p. 127.
10   D. Halberstam, *The Powers That Be*. London: Chatto & Windus 1971, pp. 225-6.
11   Conrad, op. cit., p. 135.
12   Halberstam, op. cit., pp. 700-5.
13   Ibid., p. 6.
14   E. Pearce, 'Nights Without Day'. *Radio Times*, 27 May-2 June 1989.
15   M. Cockerell, P. Hennessy & D. Walker, *Sources Close to the Prime Minister*. London: Macmillan, 1984, pp. 193-5.
16   M. Shulman, *The Ravenous Eye*. London: Cassell, 1973, pp. 116-21.
17   J. Rozenberg, 'Television Pleas'. The *Listener*, 1 June 1989. S. Doganis, 'Cine Qua Non?' Ibid.

Chapter 8
1   M. Shulman, *The Ravenous Eye*. London: Cassell, 1973, pp. 242-4.
2   Ibid., pp. 248-9.
3   *Evening Standard*, 1 June 1989.
4   M. Bland & S. Mondesir, *Promoting Yourself on Television and Radio*. London: Kogan Page, 1987, pp. 96, 13-14.
5   *Right to Reply*, Channel 4, 7 November 1987.
6   Quoted in Shulman, op. cit., p. 270.
7   Ibid.
8   *Sunday Telegraph*, 1 November 1987.
9   P. Rawlinson, *A Price Too High*. London: Weidenfeld & Nicolson, 1989, pp. 254-5.
10   D. Rintels, quoted in J. Mander, *Four Arguments for the Elimination of Television*. New York: William Morrow, 1978, p. 297.
11   Mander, op. cit., p. 298.
12   E. J. Epstein, quoted in Mander, op. cit., p. 320.
13   Mander, op. cit., p. 315.
14   S. Rushdie, *The Satanic Verses*. London: Viking Penguin, 1988, p. 402.
15   *The Times*, 9 August 1989.

Chapter 9
1   *Daily Telegraph*, 9 November 1984.
2   *Evening Standard*, 19 January 1989.

References

3   G. L. Playfair, Letter, *Daily Telegraph*, 22 November 1984.
4   M. Shulman, Letter, *Daily Telegraph*, 11 December 1984.
5   H. J. Eysenck & D. K. B. Nias, *Sex, Violence and the Media*. London: Maurice Temple Smith, 1978, p. 67.
6   D. Schorr, 'Go Get Some Milk and Cookies and Watch the Murders on Television' in R. E. Hiebert & C. Reuss, eds, *Impact of Mass Media. Current Issues*. White Plains: Longmans, 1985, ch. 19.
7   H. T. Himmelweit et al. *Television and the Child*. London: Oxford University Press, 1958, p. 56. Quoted in Eysenck & Nias, op. cit., p. 103.
8   Eysenck & Nias, op. cit., p. 154.
9   B. Gunter, *Dimensions of Television Violence*. Aldershot: Gower, 1985, p. 60. (The author is Senior Research Officer, Independent Broadcasting Authority.)
10 Eysenck & Nias, op. cit., pp. 48-9.
11 H. J. Eysenck, 'Television and the problem of violence'. *New Scientist* 12, pp. 606-7, 1960.
12 Eysenck & Nias, op. cit., p. 51.
13 Gunter, op. cit., p. 87.
14 M. Shulman, *The Ravenous Eye*. London: Cassell, 1973, p. 155.
15 Ibid., p. 191.
16 G. Barlow & A. Hill (eds), *Video Violence and Children*. London: Hodder & Stoughton, 1985, p. 136.
17 This one is not getting a free plug from me.
18 Barlow & Hill, op. cit., p. 149.
19 Ibid., pp. 152-6.
20 N. Hodgkinson, 'Videos inspire violent urge for nasty side of life.' *Sunday Times*, 3 May 1987.
21 Eysenck & Nias, op. cit., pp. 29-32.
22 Ibid., pp. 89-90.
23 Barlow & Hill, op. cit., p. 154.
24 Schorr, op. cit.

Chapter 10
1   *The Lancet*, 22 March 1986, p. 686.
2   *The Lancet*, 12 April 1986, p. 856.
3   *The Lancet*, 3 May 1986, pp. 1036-7.
4   *British Medical Journal*, 19 April 1986, p. 1073.
5   *British Medical Journal*, 11 April 1987, pp. 954-7.
6   *The Lancet*, 11 July 1987, pp. 102-3.

References

7   R. B. Ostroff et al., 'Adolescent suicides modeled after television movie.' *American Journal of Psychiatry* 142 (8) p. 989, 1985.

8   M. S. Gould & D. Shaffer, 'The impact of suicide in television movies: Evidence of imitation.' *New England Journal of Medicine* 315, pp. 690-4, 1986.

9   R. B. Ostroff & J. H. Boyd, 'Television and suicide'. *New England Journal of Medicine* 316, pp. 876-7, 1987.

10   A. Schmidtke & H. Haefner, 'The transmission of suicidal motivation and suicidal behaviour by fictional models.' *Nervenartzt* 57 (9) pp. 502-10, 1986.

11   T. A. Holding, 'Suicide and "The Befrienders" '. *British Journal of Psychiatry* 3, pp. 751-3, 1975.

12   *Sunday Express*, 30 November 1986.

13   D. P. Phillips, 'The influence of suggestion on suicide . . .' *American Sociological Review* 39, pp. 340-54, 1974.

14   R. C. Kessler et al., 'Clustering of teenage suicides after television news stories about suicide. A reconsideration.' *American Journal of Psychiatry* 145, pp. 1379-83, 1988.

15   D. P. Phillips, 'Motor vehicle fatalities increase just after publicized suicide stories.' *Science* 196, pp. 1464-5, 1977.

16   K. Lesyna & D. P. Phillips, 'Suicide and the media: Research and policy implications'. In R. Diekstra (ed.) *Preventive Strategies on Suicide*. A WHO State of the Art Publication, 1990 (in press). (Lists earlier papers by Phillips.)

17   N. Postman, *The Disappearance of Childhood*. London: W. H. Allen, 1983, pp. 108-12.

18   Ibid., p. 104.

19   Eysenck & Nias, op. cit., p. 28.

Chapter 11

1   T. M. Williams, *The Impact of Television. A Natural Experiment in Three Communities*. Orlando: Academic Press, 1986.

2   C. C. Peterson et al., 'Television viewing and imaginative problem solving during preadolescence.' *Journal of Genetic Psychology* 147 (1) pp. 61-8, 1986.

3   L. A. Tucker, 'Television, teenagers and health.' *Journal of Youth and Adolescence* 16 (5) pp. 415-26, 1987.

4   Quoted in M. Winn, *The Plug-In Drug. Television, children and the family*. Revised edition. New York/Harmondsworth: Viking Penguin, 1985, p. 80.

5   Winn, op. cit., pp. 81-3.

6   Quoted in Winn, op. cit., pp. 85-6.

7 Winn, op. cit., pp. 141-3.
8 *JAMA (Journal of the American Medical Association)* 7 October 1988, p. 1831.
9 P. A. Coleman, 'The Plug-in Drug'. *Epoch* 3 (1) pp. 2-7, 1980.
10 M. Shulman, *The Ravenous Eye.* London: Cassell, 1973, ch. 8.
11 Winn, op. cit., pp. 132-5.
12 L. Taylor & R. G. Mullan, *Uninvited Guests. The intimate secrets of television and radio.* London: Chatto & Windus, 1986, p. 61.
13 Shulman, op. cit., p.1.
14 Taylor & Mullan, op. cit., p. 61.
15 F. Pearce, 'How green are British television producers?' *Daily Telegraph*, 16 September 1989, p. iv.
16 J. Sandford, *Cathy Come Home.* London: Marion Boyars, 1976, p. 140.
17 D. Icke, 'Can radio and television become more environmentally friendly?' *Radio Times*, 26 August/1 September 1989, p. 75.

Chapter 12
1 C. Dunkley, quoted in L. Taylor & R. G. Mullan, *Uninvited Guests. The intimate secrets of television and radio.* London: Chatto & Windus, 1986, p. 196.
2 M. Shulman, *The Ravenous Eye.* London: Cassell, 1973, pp. 299-300.
3 *Denver Post*, 9 June 1974, quoted in M. Winn, *The Plug-in Drug. Television, children and the family.* Revised edition. New York/Harmondsworth: Viking Penguin, 1985, pp. 245-52.
4 Winn, op. cit., pp. 242-4.
5 Ibid., p. 253.
6 Ibid., ch. 18.
7 *Daily Telegraph*, 7 July 1989.
8 *Daily Telegraph*, 24 June 1989.
9 *JAMA (Journal of the American Medical Association)*, 7 October 1988, p. 1831.
10 *Sunday Express*, 24 March 1985.
11 Winn, op. cit., pp. 93-5.
12 N. Postman, *The Disappearance of Childhood.* London: W. H. Allen, 1983.
13 *The Times, Guardian, Daily Telegraph*, 2 August 1989, *The Times Educational Supplement*, 4 August 1989.

14   *The Times*, 3 August 1989.
15   *Daily Telegraph*, 5 August 1989.
16   A. Toffler, *The Third Wave*. London: Collins, 1980.
17   *Daily Telegraph*, 6 May 1989.
18   P. Burke, in *The Damned Art. Essays in the Literature of Witchcraft*. S. Anglo, ed., London: Routledge & Kegan Paul, 1977, p. 34.

INDEX

Index